**Lean Enterprise Institute**

Design: Thomas Skehan, Off-Piste Design
ISBN: 978-1-934109-50-2

This book includes fictional content. Names, characters, businesses,
organizations, places, events, and incidents either are the product of the
authors' imagination or are used fictitiously. Any resemblance to actual
persons (living or dead), events, or locations is strictly coincidental.

Lean Enterprise Institute, Inc.
215 First Street, Suite 300
Cambridge, MA 02142 USA
(t) 617-871-2900 • (f) 617-871-2999 • lean.org

# THE GOLD MINE
# Trilogy Study Guide

A way for teams to improve their lean practice together through reflection on the Ballé novel trilogy: *The Gold Mine, The Lean Manager,* and *Lead With Respect*

by Tom Ehrenfeld and Michael Ballé

# FOREWORD

With the Gold Mine Trilogy, authors Freddy and Michael Ballé have introduced lean principles and tools through business novels that are rich with characters facing tough problems requiring effective, sustainable countermeasures. Around the world, readers in companies large and small have used the trilogy as a guide to help them navigate their own real world situations—filled to the brim with similar problems, waste, opportunity, progress, and of course, human drama.

Hence, we offer this companion volume, the *Gold Mine Trilogy Study Guide* by Tom Ehrenfeld and Michael Ballé. The purpose of this guide is to help you use the trilogy to more effectively adopt kaizen spirit into your daily work. Our hope is that you will learn along with the books' characters to identify opportunities to move things forward in desired directions at your places of work and life. Lean principles and tools are introduced methodically to form a kind of "scaffolding" from which you can gain insights into each current situation and begin to see new horizons and futures. Invariably, as we learn to see work situations and people differently, we discover new frames with which to understand and therefore deal with the world.

The promise of this study guide is the same as that of the trilogy, which is the same as that of lean thinking itself: help us work better individually and collaboratively as we come to see the world more clearly, understand it more deeply, and deal with it more effectively. Lean is very much a journey of learning—we hope this guide helps you navigate yours.

John Shook
CEO, Lean Enterprise Institute
Cambridge, MA
October 2015

# Contents

# INTRODUCTION

Lean is not a theory; it's a practice ... You need more than
an intellectual understanding of lean tools; you need a deep
emotional commitment to solve every problem from every
single person.

  −Bob Woods

Learning lean is a personal journey. Acquiring any discipline is
tough; the work involves both ups and downs, and is prone to as many
pitfalls as successes. Do it as a flavor of the month and you'll be done
in a month. Begin with tools alone and lose hope of ever seeing lean
take root in a sustainable systematic manner. Wax eloquent on the
goodness of developing people and you'll find little engagement with
the tough challenges of making shop-floor methods work.

Lean learning must start with one person, one lesson at a time, on
the gemba, ideally with a coach who challenges you. This study guide
is designed to honor that spirit of a lean instructor who pushes you
to improve, to use tools and see problems—all the while sharing
methods to make personal improvements. A true lean coach has your
development and success in mind at all times, but also knows that if
you don't put in the effort to "learn-by-doing" for yourself, you'll
never fully understand what you're looking at.

Michael Ballé and his father Freddy have written three novels—
*The Gold Mine, The Lean Manager,* and *Lead with Respect*—that form
a trilogy of lean discovery. Why lean novels? Here's an explanation
from LEI founder Jim Womack:

> I founded LEI to teach lean methods in a situation where
> there are a lot of willing deshi (you and me as pupils) but a
> hopeless shortage of sensei (teachers with both the knowledge

and the emotional power to transform organizations.) So far we've tackled learning as an intellectual matter. In our workbooks and monthly workshops we've been teaching the technical tools you will need. But we also need to teach the emotional elements of change and for that the truths that lie in fiction are the best method at hand.

Michael and Freddy believe that learning lean goes beyond any intellectual understanding and must ultimately change behavior through direct practice. The three books were written to highlight different aspects of a lean transformation in a sequence that reflects real-life challenges encountered at the gemba. By working through one chapter at a time as a group, you will be prompted to share how the experience of the fictional characters sparks personal challenges and lessons of your own.

*The Gold Mine* is about developing problem awareness and practicing kaizen. This first novel shares the experience of working with an experienced practitioner to open your eyes to how lean systems can uncover your business challenges—even when you're surrounded by daily crises. Lean teaches you how to see: applying the tools with the right spirit teaches you to narrow down the specific improvement directions that will turn your business around. Furthermore, working with a sensei shows you how to lead from the ground up and attack these improvements with your teams on the gemba by developing their (and your) kaizen spirit.

*The Lean Manager* is the next step: lean turnaround turns into lean transformation. Having learned to see and to get kaizen started, you need to establish management systems that engage every one every day. We see how top managers support continuous improvement at the gemba by applying it everywhere: the way teams are organized, products are developed, sales are made, projects are budgeted, customers are dealt with, and much more. It also reveals the hazards of trying to fix the company at the expense of respecting and developing all people. You can use this book as a guide to making lean sustainable by establishing this mindset of engaging everyone every day as the new norm throughout a company's management system.

*Lead With Respect* continues your learning by describing the leadership required to support and develop lean systems. Lean leadership is unique in that it is not trait-based, but practice-based —and can be learned and taught. This third novel shows how to develop yourself as a lean leader and then develop others around you to create a dynamic work environment. It shows how developing others opens new avenues for improvement, and how this improvement can turn into game-changing innovation through steady kaizen.

Michael and Freddy argue that lean practice is about integrating two different flows on the gemba, the flow of work and the flow of ideas:

- Using the lean tools and integrating them progressively in a full-fledged pull system to constantly reduce lead-times and get closer to true one-piece-flow, in order to guarantee customer quality and service by looking at making products or services *one by one.*

- Revealing problems to develop people's competences and their ability to collaborate with each other by working on the practical, specific problems highlighted by the pull system. As the system gets closer to one-piece-flow, problems appear and are solved. The speed of learning increases correspondingly as initial confusion clears, generating *new ideas* to improve work methods and techniques, to take the organization beyond what it currently knows how to do.

The main purpose of the trilogy is to show lean as a full management method that achieves your goals by developing people. First you need to learn to practice kaizen, then set up management systems that will support kaizen, then develop the kind of leadership that will support, sustain, and further develop these systems to grow the company.

Never complete, never finished, always alive and adapting to its business conditions. Knowledge and mastery of lean tools is essential to such a goal. Without a deep understanding of the tools, where they apply and where they don't, what they show and how they relate to each other, the management project of lean will remain nothing more than wishful thinking.

Taken as a system of exploration, lean tools are the key to developing people's confidence in their ability to solve problems autonomously; confidence in their colleagues to do so as well; their trust in the fact that everyone can collaborate for better outcomes; pride in the improvement accomplished; and hope that together they can resolve the challenges that business throws at them.

Tools are essential to any lean journey because they are the practical methods to support true learning. They open eyes by revealing the waste in routine situations and the improvement potential in conditions that may appear normal and uninteresting. They spark problem-based learning by engaging every person in their own self-development, by getting them to solve one problem at a time and then discuss it with their boss, mentor and colleagues. They boost involvement through kaizen efforts that get teams to analyze their own work methods and propose new ones. This deeply involves team members with each other, building on the self-confidence achieved by feeling more autonomous to solve problems.

Finally, they stimulate a spirit of exploration: asking "why?" not as a deductive exercise, but as a gemba exercise of finding the best person to ask and by working across boundaries. This is the exploration tool that, with a pull system to guide it, will lead to new insights and innovation at both a local and company level.

## How to Use this Guide

This study guide is designed to support group conversations about lean practice through the sharing of stories and grappling with key questions. Please note that there are no wrong answers. This guide is not designed to test what you know to be correct, but rather to prompt you to test each other's assumptions and idea.

Because you learn lean through actual practice, this guide shares the "real" experience of our fictional characters and what they learned through trial and error. Just as they benefit from a coach who challenges and supports them through every new problem, setback, lean tool, and insight, this guide is meant to help you play this coaching role with your teammates. As you and your colleagues discuss how the stories relate to your own work, keep in mind that the discussion is meant to explore the full system of lean taught across the three books. Specific actions and events in the novels reveal how lean tools, methods, principles, and systems are all interrelated—and embedded in your lean efforts, learning, and understanding.

The guide is designed to work through the books one chapter at a time. The material is structured to support a regular cadence in which you base team discussions. Each chapter section contains:

1) A chapter summary

2) Author explanations of the significance of each chapter and how specific tools embody specific lean principles

3) Key ideas contained in the chapter

4) Reflection questions to guide your conversations

Please note that while you would ideally begin with *The Gold Mine*, followed by *The Lean Manager*, and then *Lead With Respect*, these books are standalone stories. You can easily start and learn with any one of them in any order. Enjoy!

# THE GOLD MINE

Profits are profitable—when we are able to produce consistently and on time.

–Phil Jenkinson

*Chapter One*

# PROFIT IS KING, BUT CASH RULES

*Use lean to see the full business picture (not process optimization) of how superior products, better inventory turns, and greater customer satisfaction are tied together.*

Phil Jenkinson is a young entrepreneur with a struggling business. Despite excellent products, his company faces a serious cash crisis. He turns to a sensei, Bob Woods a retired automotive executive who has successfully led many automotive supplier turnarounds. Woods has turned his back on industry to return to his first love of boats. He is brought back into the lean turnaround by his son, Mike, who as Phil's best friend, believes that his father's lean know-how and experience can help Phil save his company.

Woods initially rejects the notion that he should get involved. But eventually, he listens to Phil explain his problems, which show up as insufficient productivity and high inventory despite growing sales, all of which are now conspiring to create a cash crisis that is pushing the company to the brink of bankruptcy. Phil laments that his company is close to defaulting on its payments to suppliers, and can't pay back the high interest the banks are charging on the debts he and his partner guaranteed when they bought the ailing company.

The underlying challenge in this chapter is to understand the true nature of the crisis. In this case, it's neither a problem of sluggish sales, nor Phil's diagnosis of low profitability (although there is some of that). The primary culprit is poor cash flow due to low inventory turns and high cost of goods sold. The company has extremely weak output. If it could simply sell more products (they do have a backlog of orders) without increasing overhead or labor cost, it could postpone the immediate risk of collapse and begin to turn around its prospects.

## Author Comments

Lean is a full business outlook, not a process optimization approach. Lean is a way to think through your business in order to make the right judgment calls, based on three fundamentals:

1. Products should benefit customers through their superior performance. In Phil's case, it's an innovative component that markedly improves the product.

2. The business should generate the cash needed to sustain the further development of this benefit, through both greater distribution and further improvements.

3. Focusing on cash rather than costs is the first step to seeing your business in a lean way, and to understanding how your own operational methods either help or hinder the two previous goals.

*Learn to use the cash statement to open your eyes to the dynamic reality of the business.* Looking at cash flow opens your eyes to the relationship between your cash statement, P&L, and the balance sheet. A key lean business insight is that in order to improve bottom line profitability, you must first improve your inventory turns. Better asset utilization liberates cash to reinvest in creating greater customer value. It requires a logistics discipline that reduces costs and improves profitability.

### Key Ideas

- Change is most often triggered by crisis.
- Many companies seek rapid growth—yet aren't prepared for the problems that reaching this goal creates.
- Simply throwing cash at a problem—rather than new ideas—often amplifies problems instead of correcting them.
- "Easy" solutions often make things harder; in Phil's case, reducing inventories prevents him from delivering on time.
- Economies of scale don't add up when variety is factored in. Getting bigger and producing more variety creates challenges that are both visible and hard to see.
- Righting the ship requires the captain to get on board.

### Reflection

What lesson(s) have you learned? Please write down your answer.

Can you think of three specific examples that illustrate this learning in your own business? Please write them down.

Are you ready for change? Have you reached a point where a new approach is needed?

What is your biggest current problem?

How can you frame this problem differently? What could be the underlying causes for the most visible and present problem?

# Chapter 1: Answers, Notes, Questions

*Chapter Two*

# GOLD IN THE FLOW

*Learn to go and see at the source to understand how your gold flows in the process.*

Phil and Mike drag a reluctant Woods to the factory, where he shows them how to quickly evaluate the efficiency of a factory by observing ongoing operations. Phil eventually convinces Mike's father to help out, on the condition that Woods won't have to deal with any politics. If people don't do as he says, Woods warns, he will take a walk. Phil eagerly accepts, and they return to the plant, where they are joined by Amy Cruz, the firm's HR manager. Woods teaches them to see what he calls the "gold in the flow," or the potential value lying dormant in the plant. By carefully tracking the flow of materials and work involved in making different products, they identify the various wastes in the process and see how this affects the performance of the plant. They then focus on a specific area and look at the key metrics of quality, productivity and inventory on that part of the process, and discuss the kind of targets for improvement on this line.

The challenge here is to visualize the entire flow of materials and information through the factory, and to realize that every product that gets held up because of waste reduces the contribution of all the fixed costs of the plant to profitability. Similarly, the company is penalized by every product not shipped to the customer, which counts as inventory that is being financed by the company (parts cost, labor content, holding and handling costs).

## Author Comments

Seeing how the gold flows through the process is the essential eye-opener to start yourself on the lean thinking journey. But you have to go and look for yourself. And the best way to see what is going on is counting the components in the flow and figure out what happens to every single one of them (in service environment, this can be backlog).

The deeper point is that in order to save costs, rather than cut costs, one has to reduce inventories first by improving the flow rather than cutting costs through budget lines. Increasing inventory turns by improving specific flows will steer you towards understanding variety and productivity in new ways by focusing on what really happens at each step of the process and the real difficulties that value–adding employees face every day.

*Learn to go and see to open your eyes to facts (as opposed to reports).* Going to the gemba to see for yourself, and following a product flow continuously from delivery to customer back to the warehouse opens your eyes to customer service, productivity, and capital use.

Think of first pass yield as the money making secret: your ability to flow the product uninterrupted from customer order to delivery. To understand money leakage, red bins will show you the productivity loss resulting from non-right first time, and stagnating parts will show you capital use loss because of batch sizes or poor conveyance. Visualizing the continuous smooth flow of value opens your eyes to how profitable you could really be.

### Key Ideas

- Many problems that present themselves as financial shortfalls and strategic deficiencies are in fact outcomes of basic operational incapability—and must be addressed where they occur rather than after the fact or in a conference room.
- These global business problems can only be understood by focusing on what is *actually* happening—the specific details of the work, which must be carefully observed where it takes place.
- Moving from batch production to a flow of value to the customer reveals which actions create value, which do not, and point to ways that excess inventory hide problems, tie up cash, and prevent learning.
- To see the process, you need to count parts and people on the shop floor, one by one. You need to get directly involved to open your eyes. In lean terms, you need to "see with your feet and think with your hands."
- To understand the system you must disaggregate what you make/sell rather than work from the top down. For example, product variety and customer demand are the key to understanding what happens in the plant.
- Quality improvement is the real source of productivity, but hard to see at first, so a more obvious starting point is understanding inventory.
- Cost saving is different from cost cutting.
- You can see a lot just by looking.

### Equation

$$\text{Lead Time} = \frac{\text{Total WIP}}{\text{Production Rate}}$$

## Reflection

What lesson(s) have you learned? Please write down your answer.

Can you think of three specific examples that illustrate this learning in your own business? Please write them down.

Can you trace the entire value stream from the value you deliver to your customer, all the way back to your raw materials or basic services?

Can you see instances where the flow of material and information is interrupted, and where work that creates no value takes place?

Can you start to calculate how much this costs you?

How many different ways does this cost you?

## Chapter 2: Answers, Notes, Questions

*Chapter Three*

# TAKT TIME

*Learn to use takt time to understand what and when the customer needs, and to understand the capacity needs of your business.*

In order to understand the basic rhythm of how the factory produces finished products for the customer, Woods asks Phil to use stopwatches to time the operators as they work. This triggers an angry battle at the plant where production manager Dave Koslowsky accuses them of using lean as a way to fire people. Phil promises that no one will be fired as a result of this work.

Woods explains that the purpose of determining this rhythm, defined as takt time, of customer demand: doing so will unlock the productivity challenges created by what lean experts call muda, mura, and muri. These three wastes all arise from unnecessary variation in the way things are made, which directly causes nonvalue-adding work, overburden, and unevenness.

He argues that the first step to lean improvement comes through creating basic process stability in the system, a job that can begin by stopping defects as they occur. To accomplish this he suggests a "red bin" system to isolate non-conformity at every workstation; and he adds to this by discussing the impact of variation on productivity. He asks Phil and his team to start reducing the variation in the operator's cycles before tackling more detailed inefficiency.

Woods explains that the purpose of this work is to develop a clear idea for every one of what work—good or bad—means. He asks Phil, How do people know they are doing the job right? How do they know they are not creating problems up or down the line? How do they know what to do when they encounter a problem?

## Author Comments

In true sensei fashion, Woods does not lecture or explain, but sets practical exercises for Phil and Amy to figure things out through practice—to learn-by-doing. His guidelines are structured around customer satisfaction, just-in-time delivery, and built-in quality.

But seeing the potential for improvement in routine work is only half the battle. The second key point Woods is trying to make is that it's all about people. This is not a technical process issue to solve, but a leadership issue. Phil needs to learn to be a different kind of leader. Again, the sensei does not explain or discuss theory, but steers Phil to work more closely with Gloria and her team so that they understand the challenge, the objectives, and they figure out how to get there.

Beyond extracting immediate productivity gains, Phil has to *demonstrate* his commitment to change and to start building trust. Woods knows that this can't be intellectual posturing. Such attitude changes must be lived from the gut, hence the sink or swim approach. All this time, he knows what changes he expects from Phil, but doesn't know whether Phil will learn to swim and become a lean leader, or sink and continue to blame his environment, his engineers, and ultimately his employees for his troubles. Only doing can tell.

*Learn to calculate takt time to open your eyes to the real capacity needs of your business.* A rough and ready calculation of takt time, even in situations where it only applies approximately, will immediately make you see whether you are right-sized to deliver to customer demand or whether your attribution of resources creates many of the problems you're trying to solve in the first place. Instead of running any process at full speed to go through a batch "productively," takt time calculations, overall and by product, will open your eyes to where resources are really needed and for what, and what would be right-sized capital and labor use.

## Key Ideas

- Takt time is the "North Star" that regulates production processes in any work setting.
- Moving from batch to flow production must be paired with a shift from having materials pushed upstream at the operator's convenience to being pulled when they are needed.
- The process of understanding the *details* of the real work enables you to determine the ideal number of operators on the line; which trains everyone to identify variation; which enables you to move on to analyzing value-adding work versus non-value-adding work.
- For workers, all activity is work—whether value-added or not—and having a method for distinguishing between the two enables progress to be made.
- Variation caused by man, machine, material, or method is a major problem regarding performance and must be dealt with.
- Takt time, like all lean tools, exists for a deeper reason. Its purpose is to help identify the waste that is created through flawed processes.
- Once waste is identified, it can be addressed and eliminated through a better understanding of how the work is done.

## Equations & Graphics

$$\text{Takt Time} = \frac{\text{Available Daily Production Time}}{\text{Daily Customer Demand}}$$

$$\text{Number of Operators} = \frac{\text{Total Work Content}}{\text{Takt Time}}$$

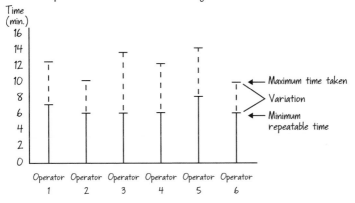

**Operator Balance Chart with Cycle Time Variation**

Maximum time taken
Variation
Minimum repeatable time

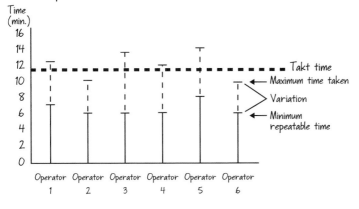

**Operator Balance Chart with Takt Time**

Takt time
Maximum time taken
Variation
Minimum repeatable time

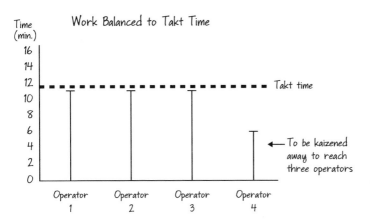

**Work Balanced to Takt Time**

Takt time
To be kaizened away to reach three operators

### Reflection

What lesson(s) have you learned? Please write down your answer.

Can you think of three specific examples that illustrate this learning in your own business? Please write them down.

Can you identify where and how your operational system is causing you to create waste?

Do you have a mechanism such as takt time that connects your work directly to customer value?

Who is your customer? How does every person on your team relate their work to the delivery of value to internal and external customers?

### Chapter 3: Answers, Notes, Questions

*Chapter Four*

# STANDARDIZE WORK

*Create standardized work and use 5S to see how your work flows and take ownership for your work area.*

Phil, Amy (HR director) and Mike meet up with Bob Woods at his yacht. They discuss the experiment of taking people off the production line and Amy shares that it has met some success. They explore the challenge of how to enable work that is good—so that it can be better. Woods asks: What's a good operator? What exactly characterizes someone doing quality work? This leads to a discussion about standardized work, which he defines as always doing the same operations in the same order, using the 5S exercise as a tool to support this approach. Woods goes on to explain that creating and applying standard work *does not* limit or constrain individuals, but instead serves as the basis for continuous involvement and improvement.

Building the 5S discipline is a practical way of introducing standard work, Woods explains, because it enables managers to suggest standardized cleanup sheets, which is something people will be familiar with. Moreover, it helps operates accept responsibility of their own workstations rather than have it be imposed upon them. To command responsibility is to fundamentally contradict it.

## Author Comments

For people to feel confident about their work, they first need to know what they know. Standardized work is a key technique to clarifying in one's mind the sequence of tasks one should carry out to successfully achieve an activity, as well as the quality criteria at each step.

*Standardized work opens your eyes to the fluidity of work, and 5S teaches employees to organize their work areas autonomously.* Standardized work is not about imposing a single way of working on all workers, but rather it's about building their individual knowledge and self-awareness of how they do a job. 5S is a key technique for helping them take control of their work environment by eliminating ambiguity and sources of variation through proper organization and maintenance of components and tools. The aim of 5S is to give workers a self-development tool to "own" their workplace, to create standardized work, and from there on, kaizen.

Standardized work guarantees delivery, quality, and efficiency, but it can only be achieved locally according to local circumstances. 5S is a thinking tool to consider how to best organize the environment to achieve the smooth, regular flow of standardized, productive work.

## Key Ideas

- The key to productivity is the stability of the work cycle.
- To have stable work cycles, people must feel confident as they move from one step to the next.
- Standard work is the basis for improvement and involvement.
- Standard work cannot be imposed on people; in fact operators must, with the help of their team leader, create their own standard work based on the best and most intuitive way to get it done.
- The fundamental purpose of standard work is to distinguish immediately what is OK from what is NOT-OK.

## Reflection

What lesson(s) have you learned? Please write down your answer.

Can you think of three specific examples that illustrate this learning in your own business? Please write them down.

Are you familiar with the basics of 5S, and the intent behind it?

Do you have standard work in your job? If no, why not?

Does your team leader (boss) understand your standard work?

Does your standard work change? If so, what triggers revisions?

## Chapter 4: Notes, Answers, Questions

*Chapter Five*

# IT'S ALL ABOUT THE PEOPLE

*Create stable teams of 5 to 6 people with a team leader to create a structure for group learning at the gemba.*

Phil and Amy discover, to both their delight and consternation, that running workshops releases huge amounts of potential and gains —and years of bottled-up employee complaints. Managers have been forced to realize that operators have been complaining about causes of variation in their work for years. Because management never paid attention, they lowered their expectations—which set both parties on a cycle of failure.

When Phil and Amy ask Woods how to build on their gains, he introduces the key principle of kaizen—continuous improvement that is "all about the people." Using the example of how a boat skipper leads his team, he details a system of teamwork and coaching in which the team leader guides and supports his group of workers. The greatest challenge in lean is having an explicit approach to coaching, developing, and leading employees in daily improvement through the work at hand. This means shifting supervisors from the traditional role of creating work calendars, finding missing parts, doing general fire-fighting, etc., to seeing themselves as mentors who develop work standards and train workers to use standard work as the basis for involvement and continuous improvement.

Woods defines the team leader role as someone picked from the workers, not a hierarchal boss so much as a person deeply familiar with the work at hand who can make sure that hourly production targets are achieved by helping solve all the little mishaps which happen in day-to-day operations.

## Author Comments

The unfortunate lesson of much "coaching" and improvement work is that change is not necessarily an improvement. Kaizen has to be change for the better. Change never occurs in a vacuum. We all learn within the context of our peer groups and teams.

What teams do is produce norms according to the direction given by their leader. The challenge is to harness this behavior to support teams to solve their daily performance problems and to improve how they work together.

The team leader's role is essential both as a reference point for standards and as a driver of small step improvement, to teach team members how to better coordinate their work together, and leverage team performance. Team leaders must balance a solid knowledge of the work with an easy manner, so that team members look to them for guidance and which attitude to adopt in uncertain situations. It's all about people: teams and their team leaders are the focus of kaizen.

*Learn to use stable teams of 5 or 6 people with a team leader to see how you learn and create value at the gemba.* How are employees organized? Looking to see if there are stable teams with a team leader shows you whether the workplace is organized by learning. People learn within teams, when they are responsible for their production equipment and work on familiar products.

The alternative, staffing people according to demand, as with airline attendant crews, requires extremely defined processes and rigorous discipline, without much possibility for improvement. Looking at whether each employee is part of a stable team, spotting who the team leader is and wondering whether the frontline manager is encouraging (or discouraging) learning gives an instant picture of how fast the area will learn and improve.

## Key Ideas

- The essence of continuous improvement (kaizen) is small step improvements from everyone every day, as a way of building in employee involvement.
- The primary role of lean managers is to develop people through the use of lean tools and methods.
- Every operator is part of a stable team led by a leader whose role is to ensure that everyone masters standard work.
- Produce people before producing parts.

## Graphics

| Production Analysis Board | | | |
|---|---|---|---|
| Hour | Plan | Good parts | Comments |
| 1 | | | |
| 2 | | | |
| 3 | | | |
| 4 | | | |
| 5 | | | |
| 6 | | | |
| 7 | | | |
| 8 | | | |

$$\frac{\text{Good parts}}{\text{Number of operators} \times \text{hours}} =$$

**Reflection**

What lesson(s) have you learned? Please write down your answer.
Can you think of three specific examples that illustrate this learning in your own business? Please write them down.
Are you truly involved with your own work improvement?
How?
What role does your boss or team plan in daily improvement?
What visual or other tools support your team's performance?

**Chapter 5: Answers, Notes, Questions**

*Chapter Six*

# LEVEL TO PULL

*Use your pull system and improved flexibility to uncover and address problems as they occur.*

Mike, Phil, and Amy reflect on the success they have seen from operators building the mechanisms on sub-assembly lines in terms of increasing daily production with the same amount of resources, while consistently hitting new production targets. Expecting a pat on the back from their sensei, they are instead a bit miffed when he drags them to a local supermarket.

Woods wants to push them to be far more ambitious in reducing their inventory, to move from a smaller amount of work-in-process (WIP), to a fundamentally different mindset—from batch to flow, or level to pull. This lesson involves a complicated discussion of how much WIP should be held at each cell for the process, since lean processes always stress flow over storing excess material.

The light bulb goes off for Amy when she recalls her experience working in a fast food restaurant and the use of shop stock. The significance of this approach has to do with creating the proper tension in the system for regular production in a way that contains maximum flexibility, responsiveness, and stability. The system is lean because it pulls on a controlled stock and delivers goods to customers just-in-time, while the staff resources in the kitchen vary according to the demand at various hours of the day. Woods explains how to use takt time to build a leveled production program, which pulls continuously on the production cell.

## Author Comments

There is no lean without pull. Regardless of your field, without pull you'll keep using tools and skirting lean without ever discovering its profound insights. A pull system is a combination of takt time-based leveled planning, end-to-end kanban, poka-yokes, and andon. Whether in industrial production, engineering, service or software development, learning to pull work is a key lean learning activity.

The dinner lecture by Stephen McAllister shares a fundamental lean insight. Reducing batch size is essential to accelerating flows, but so is increasing the frequency of deliveries. If a pull system picks up finished work every twenty minutes, it creates the tension that will reveal detailed problems. If you only deliver work when the full load is complete you can hide many mishaps and reworks. The tempo of twenty minute pickups creates a dynamic environment in which people can see problems more quickly—often one at a time—and learn to improve what they do. Precision in logistics is the key that opens the door to lean thinking and profitability. Without it, kaizen and coaching efforts can often go round in circles and fix non-issues whilst avoiding real problems.

*Pull frequently to open your eyes to the real problems people experience, and practice quick changeovers to see the real flexibility of your equipment and system.* Stabilizing the number of products or services to perform each day according to customer averages is the key to stabilizing a learning environment. A stable plan with regular achievement objectives leads to seeing what typical problems people face every day. Reducing batches to better mix demand on the line will reveal technical problems at the time of work change.

Increasing flexibility is the key to better understanding work. Increasing the frequency of pick-ups will reveal how difficult it often is for employees to achieve their targets. So many manpower, machine, materials, and method hiccups prevent a steady, efficient work pace. This will open your eyes to the true potential of kaizen.

## Key Ideas

- For a just-in-time system to deliver lean results in terms of labor cost and capital utilization, the pull signal must be "leveled" as much as possible, both in mix and volume. If you do not adjust your system accordingly your team will never be able to reap the cash, labor and capital benefits from just-in-time techniques such as kanban.
- Once again, the technical challenges of a lean method must be mastered, but not as a mere tool—understanding the underlying purpose of the tool in the system matters most.
- Just like at IEP, many companies will find that early shop floor gains often reveal newer and even more challenging problems. And that these new challenges demand even greater commitment from managers and willingness to press on despite new setbacks and the possible emergence of simmering tensions.

## Graphics

### Customer demand for Industrial Extreme Vacuum (IEV) product

| Product | Weekly demand | Daily demand | Takt time based on 450 min./day |
|---------|---------------|--------------|----------------------------------|
| STR | 100 | 20 | 22.5 min. |
| QST-1 | 55 | 11 | 40.9 min. |
| QST-2 | 50 | 10 | 45 min. |
| DG | 20 | 4 | 112.5 min. |
| Total | 225 | 45 | 10 min. |

## Level build schedule for IEV products

| Time | 10 min. | 10 min. | 10 min. | 10 min. | 10 min. | 10 min. | 10 min. | 10 min. | 10 min. | 10 min. | 10 min. |
|---|---|---|---|---|---|---|---|---|---|---|---|
| Conveyor | STR | QST-1 | STR | QST-2 | STR | QST-1 | STR | QST-2 | STR | DG | STR |

## Updated delivery schedule for IEV products

| | | Before | After |
|---|---|---|---|
| STR mechanism | Parts | 40/day | 80/day |
| | People | 6 | 8 |
| QST-1, QST-2 and DG mechanisms | Parts | 70/day | 78/day |
| | People | 12 | 7 + 1 |

## Reflection

What lesson(s) have you learned? Please write down your answer (*see page 32*).

Can you think of three specific examples that illustrate this learning in your own business? Please write them down.

Does your work flow?

Is it regulated by the pace of customer demand?

Have your discussions to date given you the ability to "see" the value stream and track products along it, which helps identify waste and standardize operations?

If so, what else can help you level your production to ensure pull?

Do your downstream processes obtain precisely what they need when they need it?

Are your upstream activities as efficient as possible?

# Chapter 6: Answers, Notes, Questions

*Chapter Seven*

# KANBAN RULES

*Use kanban to visualize the information flow of work and tie this work to real customer demand.*

As Phil and Amy continue to see huge improvements in the way operators and processes work—from a cleaner and better organized factory to traction with methods like takt time and flow. Still, during a plant visit, Woods stubbornly questions why they have created a massive conveyor to carry parts. He points out logistics issues that are interrupting flow. This triggers a discussion about kanban.

Kanban is the key tool for kaizen. Woods explains how to establish a kanban, shares basic rules, and leads an inquiry into kanban's true purpose. Creating a work environment where kaizen and standardized work can flourish requires visual management so that people can distinguish at one glance the difference between a normal situation with kanban cards flowing as expected, and an abnormal situation where material or kanban cards don't flow.

Woods asks Phil and Amy to visualize the entire flow in the plant, from the truck preparation area in dispatch, to the shop stock at the conveyor and at the mechanism lines. He also introduces the heijunka board, which shows material handlers how to do the picking from the conveyor's shop stock into the truck preparation area.

Phil and Amy continue to struggle with how long it takes for new practice to take hold. A fight with logistics manager Kevin Lorentz reveals that everyone must consider logistics when tackling issues such as flow, Woods commits to a deeper engagement to help out.

## Author Comments

End-to-end kanban is a physical sign of lean thinking: no container moves without a kanban instruction. We can all see easily the flow of material, but kanban visualizes the *information flow* that controls the material flow. The deep insight underlying kanban is that all material should be part of a dynamic circuit—like blood running through the body—rather than static accumulations. Everything moves continuously, and when a circuit fails you react quickly to address the problem. Kanban requires that all functions work together to make the kanban run, which in turn builds-up teamwork.

Kanban is a great measure to see: 1) whether the company is working on the right things right now to serve customer demand and 2) how well teamwork functions across functional departments.

*Learn to use kanban to open your eyes to the work employees are doing right now and to see how this relates to real customer demand.* No work should happen without a kanban instruction that says "do this now." With this ideal in mind, we can think about how to establish kanban signals in any situation, whether production, engineering or service.

Kanban is the visualization of information flow—which is much harder to grasp than the obvious material flow of production or service. Kanban will open your eyes to the fact that people can be working very hard at something that doesn't help with immediate customer delivery, without any notion of what it means to succeed.

By using kanban you can refocus work with the fundamental questions: "Who are we doing this job for? How will we know we've done it successfully? How close are we to handling one job at a time from start to finish? What obstacles do we encounter to completing one job fully, successfully and right when the customer needs it?"

## Key Ideas

- Achieving flow requires all aspects of production (including logistics and IT) to work together.
- Kanban is a tool to schedule production in a way that problems appear immediately, at the point of cause, so that they can be resolved right away.
- Kanban's purpose is not to relieve production from worry about logistics. Kanban's purpose is to fail every time the flow gets out of standard condition.
- Kanban is a kaizen tool, and not the other way around.
- Kanban has deep and wide-ranging applications.

## Graphics

### Leveling (Heijunka) Box with kanban cards

| Products | 8:30 | 9:00 | 9:30 | 10:00 | 10:45 | 11:15 | 11:45 | 12:15 | 13:45 | 14:15 | 14:45 | 15:15 | 16:00 | 16:30 | 17:00 | 17:30 |
|---|---|---|---|---|---|---|---|---|---|---|---|---|---|---|---|---|
| STR |  | / |  | / | / | / |  | / | / |  | / | / |  | / |  | / |
| STR-X | / |  | / |  | / |  | / |  | / |  | / |  | / |  | / |  |
| QST-1A | / |  |  |  | / |  |  | / |  |  | / |  |  |  |  | / |
| QST-1B |  |  | / |  |  |  |  |  |  |  |  | / |  |  |  |  |
| QSR-1C |  | / |  |  | / |  |  |  | / |  |  |  | / |  |  |  |
| QST-2X |  |  | / |  |  |  | / |  |  |  | / |  |  |  | / |  |
| QST-2Y | / |  |  | / |  |  | / |  |  | / |  |  | / |  |  | / |

### Reflection

What lesson(s) have you learned? Please write down your answer.

Can you think of three specific examples that illustrate this learning in your own business? Please write them down.

Does your team have a form of kanban?

Does your kanban reveals the sources of waste and the health of your processes?

If you lack a formal kanban system, what mechanisms do you have for gauging how well your work flows, how stable it is, what causes defects, and what connects it to customer value?

### Chapter 7: Answers, Notes, Questions

*Chapter Eight*

# GEMBA ATTITUDE

*Commit to the gemba attitude of going where the work occurs, observing carefully, and solving problems where they occur.*

Phil and Amy bring Woods and Mike to observe the current state of operations, seeking ways to build on the progress they've made with the use of kanban to help with the challenges of creating flow. Woods instructs them to observe the shop floor activity carefully—to observe without commenting or filtering until they begin to see with greater awareness. He helps them identify new challenges for maintaining the equipment; new ways to improve operating conditions.

Beyond the specific tools such as quick changeover and TPM, Woods argues that the heart of lean is teaching and practicing rigorous problem-solving at the place where work happens with the full engagement and coaching of team leaders and managers. He shares the *five why* exercise made famous by Taichii Ohno, urging them to see it not as a rote catechism but a way of thinking with others, as a means of revealing the sources of problems.

"Seeing can't be taken for granted," Woods says, "It's an attitude. It's a commitment to go to the 'real place'—the gemba—and figure out what is happening for real and not be content with what sounds likely. When in doubt, go and see what is going on."

Woods demonstrates a "just-do-it" example of the lean mindset. He organizes an impromptu build of the cabinet assembly cell, working with the operators and shop-floor technicians. This sets off a battle with between Phil and his partner Matt about the depth of their commitment to total lean implementation—another test of gemba attitude.

## Author Comments

Gemba attitude means: go and see, clear your mind and think about what you see. This often means abandoning the illusion that issues can be solved globally—once and for all. Gemba attitude means accepting:

1) Large problems are unknowable in their entirety so they will be discovered from change point to change point.

2) Each change is worked with people, to both engage them and benefit from their ideas and involve them so that they'll support and sustain the changes on their own.

3) We act ourselves into understanding, rather than understand ourselves into thinking.

Without a gemba attitude, lean tools can easily be subverted by commonplace corporate practices that sap their potential for real insight and developing mutual trust. Value-stream mapping or A3 problem solving become disconnected meeting room activities, with no grip on the workplace and no valuable learning with employees.

*Learn to stand in a circle and observe for more than ten minutes, to open your eyes to the waste created by your method of operation of any process.* Then try to improve things immediately, see how that works, and think of the next steps. By leading teams into immediate action, whether on flow, safety, TPM, etc., you can lead by example on the ground, while also assessing the strength and weaknesses of your products, people, and processes firsthand, thereby finding out what you need to change in your organization.

## Key Ideas

- Stand in the circle until you see. Stand even longer.
- To obtain lasting results after initial quick wins from tools, one must follow the *five why* exercise rigorously, so as to always resolve the fundamental cause of any problem.
- Every gemba problem is an opportunity for improvement. Every process in every setting must be owned by the operators.

## Reflection

What lesson(s) have you learned? Please write down your answer (*see page 40*).

Can you think of three specific examples that illustrate this learning in your own business? Please write them down.

What problems and battles do you see your lean work creating?

How do you plan (what are your next steps) on handling them?

Can you apply the *five why* approach to one of your current tough challenges?

Are you really walking the walk or just talking the talk?

Where can you take these lessons directly to your gemba and learn by doing rather than simply discussing?

# Chapter 8: Answers, Notes, Questions

*Chapter Nine*

# THE HEIJUNKA WAY

*Map your material and information flow on a large scale to see how you can one day reach one-piece-flow.*

Phil begins to face a greater set of systematic problems revealed by the success of shop floor progress. Woods shares his intent to quit, so that Phil will learn to lead the lean work himself. Phil persuades him to remain as an advisor. Later when Phil shares continued challenges of enlisting key players in a useful way (for example, the way they are seeing the use of an MRP system for the plant), Woods challenges him to set his managerial sights higher.

Woods suggests that a useful way to see current problems (like leveling the relationship between JIT techniques and MRP, or protecting the production process from volume variations in customer orders, or the continued challenges to variation in the production process) is to apply value-stream-mapping on a large scale approach.

Woods essentially recognizes and validates the progress that Phil has led at his company. Phil must now integrate the lean approach within all the activities of his company. Woods suggests that mapping material and information flow can aid this enormously. It will help him to maintain both a big picture outlook and a detailed vision of the plant—at the same time. The visual tools show the plant's processes as a continuous flow, and enlarge the vision to include customer and supplier effects on the total supply chain.

## Author Comments

As you learn to use lean tools to better understand how your department works and the cost overruns created by your own operations methods, you will develop an increased appreciation of the structuring power of takt time and the need for leveling, or heijunka.

Heijunka has two dimensions: first, leveling customer demand to avoid the bullwhip effect of magnifying small random changes throughout the value chain, and second, dividing and mixing batches in order to increase the flexibility of work and smooth the flow, with the intent of one day reaching true one-piece-flow.

A good sign that you are making progress as a lean leader is that you devote increasing resources into leveling production plans, mixing production schedules, reducing batch sizes, and increasing the frequency of pull through kanban, better deal with demand *now*!

Forcing yourself to improve flexibility in mix and volume will immediately highlight how investment decisions in job roles and equipment type help (or hinder) flow and overall productivity, or by contrast, encourage piece rate and rigid job specialization to optimize spot output at the expense of customer outcomes.

*Learn to plan a steady demand over short periods to open your eyes to see how frequent re-programming degrades performance.* Flexibility is only possible, however, in a work environment protected from muri (overburden) and mura (stop-and-go). The further you are on your lean journey the more you realize how leveling customer demand is critical to being able to deliver on time one product at a time. By trying to average customer demand over short and long period and distinguishing the base rate of the pace of demand from spot up-and-downs, you get to learn what demand is really like and how to protect delivery processes from flash floods, in order to work with them to improve their flexibility.

## Key Ideas

- A crucial part of everyone's lean journey is to shift from being a leader/follower (with a sensei) to a teacher/mentor coach of others. (One can always have a sensei to be sure; but one must eventually wean reliance on a master for lessons.)
- Leadership must see and share the "big picture" with all.
- The purpose of mapping is to focus attention on the work itself, at all levels.
- Lean turnarounds are always systems turnarounds—meaning that change in one portion of the system creates changes (often seen as problems) in everything that interacts with this portion.
- Regardless of where you start (motion kaizen, then equipment kaizen, etc), eventually you will find that point kaizen is futile if not integrated into full system kaizen.
- Having a way to see the full material and information flow, and understand the barriers to flow, is key to continuing and sustaining lean practice.

## Reflection

What lesson(s) have you learned? Please write down your answer (*see page 44*).

Can you think of three specific examples that illustrate this learning in your own business? Please write them down.

Who is your lean sensei?

Do you rely too much on your sensei right now?

Are you ready to teach others?

Where do you see your lean progress creating problems with people, teams, and divisions, with whom you interact?

## Chapter 9: Notes, Answers, Questions

*Chapter Ten*

# KAIZEN FOREVER

*Honor the kaizen spirit by using your lean practice to create a culture of continued improvements in smaller and smaller details over time.*

The news that Amy is leaving sparks another cycle of progress, setbacks, tough sensei love, and humbling new insights from Phil that keep the lean journey stumbling forward. He reaches out once more to Woods for help in framing his newest set of managerial and systemic challenges, and agrees to host a plant tour by Woods' sensei, who is visiting from Japan. The sensei drills Phil on his deficiencies regarding built-in quality, or jidoka. He doesn't see enough physical evidence of tools such as andon, autonomation, poka-yoke, and other techniques that support the key TPS pillar of building in quality.

Woods identifies the challenges of creating a sustainable lean system. First, one must have a system in place; second, a leader has to find and develop people to lead within that system. The path to becoming lean is unending.

Phil has in fact reached a dramatic new level of company performance—which has uncovered a host of new problems by clearing away more waste. He finally learns to accept this as the natural course of lean learning, and commits himself to continuous personal growth. He realizes that regardless of how much expertise he may gain, he must remain a student who is open and devoted to the lean voyage of discovery.

## Author Comments

*Lean thinking starts with quality and ends with quality (and then repeats).* Kaizen establishes the link between the customer experience and the detailed knowledge of OK versus NOT-OK in every task.

A fascinating aspect of the kaizen spirit is that there is no end to the benefits it provides. The deeper the understanding, the greater the opportunities to find true innovation in mundane improvements. Practicing kaizen not only makes the company more productive today but opens new ways to satisfy customers tomorrow. But this rests on the ability of leaders to sustain the kaizen spirit, day in and day out, and to see the company as never complete, never finished, never ripe.

The lean system offers clear targets for further improvements:

• *Better satisfy customers*: what do customers really care about? How can I better help them support their chosen lifestyle as opposed to impose the burden of my own internal processes on them? How can I both improve basic performance and propose new features they'll actually use?

• *Improve built-in quality* by seeking to spot defects ever closer to where they're being created, stop the process sooner and react more vigorously to every issue, stimulating deeper thinking by asking "why?" again and again.

• *Improve the just-in-time level* by constantly reducing lead-times. Every company has a just-in-time level, whether several years for construction, several month for equipment, several minutes for high volume products or half-a second for an Internet search engine. In any situation, ask yourself, How can I cut this lead time in half?

• *Involve teams more deeply* in devising their own standardized work and studying their own work methods and coming up with kaizen ideas. In any workplace, how many devices where invented by the team itself? How many suggestions were implemented? How can you double both?

Kaizen forever means developing the capability to integrate the insights from kaizen in the day-to-day running of the department. This requires a special kind of leader who will 1) spur kaizen through specific, pragmatic challenges, and then 2) learn from kaizen initiatives and change their own work to build on the insights coming out of the kaizen efforts.

*Set up andon to see the countless disturbances and interruptions that employees face in their routine jobs.* Spotting defects immediately as they are created opens a window on how to truly understand technical processes. Stopping work at every defect reveals what people understand about quality from the customer's point of view, and about Ok versus not-OK in their own work. Making automatic devices to signal and stop when tools are no longer in good conditions or when materials are not as good as expected makes you truly see how you handle work. Andon is the ultimate key of forever kaizen because it deepens process capability by capturing intelligence in smaller and smaller details.

### Key Ideas

- Lean systems will always contain a creative tension that drives systematic, divisional, cellular, and individual learning and growth.
- The goal of continuous improvement is continuous improvement.
- Use the system to grow your people and develop *esprit de corps*.
- You must always build quality into your products and services, not inspect it in.

### Reflection

What lesson(s) have you learned? Please write down your answer.

Can you think of three specific examples that illustrate this learning in your own business? Please write them down.

What is your next challenge?

Who will you share your lean learning with?

### Chapter 10: Answers, Notes, Questions

# THE LEAN MANAGER

Lean management is about creating a system to make people think. It's about making people before making things. And better thinking leads to better products.

–Bob Woods

*Chapter One*

# CUSTOMERS FIRST

*Embrace your problems and orient your value to customers by making complaints visible and using red bins to capture the waste in your processes.*

Plant manager Andy Ward can't believe his plant is in danger. His background as a consultant, and then continuous improvement officer, have led to a career at the automotive division of Alnext, where he has been the plant manager of the Vaudon factory in France for several years. Now he hears word that the new CEO Phil Jenkinson, intends to shutter his operation.

Since Phil was made CEO by the private equity group that acquired Alnext, he has made dramatic changes throughout: selling corporate HQ and relocating everyone in plants, sending all corporate-wide improvement specialists to line functions, selling certain plants and product lines, re-structuring supply chain operations, and much more.

During his visit to Vaudon, Phil drills Andy on his plant's poor quality, inattention to safety, and on his ignorance of key metrics related to financial goals tied to operational numbers. He tells Andy that unless he can reduce plant costs, while boosting quality and delivery performance, he will either replace Andy or shut down the plant.

Later, Phil shares that what he's really looking for is *right attitude*: plants where employees are contributing to customer value through the use of quality and process improvement, and managers are supporting this actively every day, in every way. He tells Andy that, "You are all the help the plant needs." He agrees that if Andy can fix the quality problems, eliminate customer complaints and missed deliveries, he will consider a different course of action.

## Author Comments

Staff structures are excellent at solving the top problems in the Pareto when there is a crisis, but this is not enough to deliver superior performance for customers; all issues count, even the rare, unlikely ones. Quality problems are a reflection of how well processes are understood and under control, which in turn drives profitability; quality drives sales and first pass yield drives productivity.

Attacking all quality issues requires that production take responsibility for serving customers and solving its own problems: processes designed by staff experts or computer systems are enough to churn out output, but don't guarantee outcome—this needs fighting on every quality and service to customers every day both to serve them better and to develop a deeper understanding of what it is we do.

As a CEO Phil tries to convey the same message he learned, the hard way, from Bob Woods in *The Gold Mine*: you can't administrate operations and keep running things hoping they will deliver results. You've got to roll up your sleeves and get into the fray and work with the people to understand issues and get teams to learn how to fix them.

As an engineer, Phil grasps that it's all about the product, and forces the entire company to refocus on product quality and delivery rather than worry about maintaining its internal processes and systems. This comes as a shock to senior management who sees the status quo being strongly challenged by the CEO. As a plant manager, Andy is caught in the crossfire of political battles about what should be the shape of the entire company in the future, which is a position that many operational managers are familiar with. In taking the initiative to defend his position, he shows potential and initiates the learning relationship with Phil. The CEO's problem is indeed that learning goes two ways: the teacher promises to teach but the learner has to promise to learn, and, as it turns out, Phil is short of operational managers with any interest to learn from him.

*List all customer complaints visually to see how your processes generate waste for customers, and learn to use red bins to open your eyes to the quality issues that operators face daily.* Visiting customers to understand their complaints is the only way to truly grasp how customers use our product or service to support their lifestyles and in what conditions. The producer can't help looking at products or service generically: one size fits a full segment.

By going and seeing firsthand what makes customers complain, we can grasp what customers are trying to achieve, and how our products and services help or hinder them. This case by case experience is essential to building up a mental image of how to improve products and services right now in order to offer more attractive products and services in the next development cycle, and thus sustainably grown the business. At the workplace, red bins are a key tool to see how we translate our understanding of customer value into OK/NOT-OK quality for routine work. Red bins are a focal point to get management and employees to converge on what gives meaning to work: supporting customers in what they want to do by mastering work processes.

### Key Ideas

- A lean company is one where everybody contributes directly to adding value to customers.
- Kaizen cannot be taught as an abstract exercise by high-potential specialists on a drive-by basis; it must be practiced by everyone everyday where the work is done. Production, sales, etc must all take responsibility for their own quality.
- Put customers first by getting line management to own and fix quality and delivery problems.

### Reflection

What lesson(s) have you learned? Please write down your answer.

Can you think of three specific examples that illustrate this learning in your own business? Please write them down.

Can you see the link between your work and the current business state that is shared to you by company leaders?

### Chapter 1: Answers, Notes, Questions

*Chapter Two*

# EVERYBODY, EVERY DAY

*Engage every person in kaizen learning activities led by a local team leader to establish autonomous problem-solving.*

Andy attacks his plant's problems, determined to follow Phil's marching orders as literally as possible. His new commitment to reviewing every lost-time incident immediately reduces the reported number in half. His new approach of talking directly, in-depth, with employees about shop-floor and related problems, uncovers tensions, attitudes, and information he had previously been unaware of.

Phil continues to press him on matters like visiting a customer's line to better understand quality issues and develop a better relationship. He insists that there will be no further investment on existing processes, which must be improved through kaizen alone. Investments will be limited to new products and processes alone. Furthermore, he reveals that the purpose of this policy is to generate learning through the use of the PDCA cycle by the operators and team leaders.

Andy lobbies for the new approach with both his management team and the shop-floor operators. First step: red containers to capture every non-conforming part produced in every cell. Initially, these exercises fail to gain traction, as they lack visible managerial support, and serve more to air longstanding grievances.

A visit from Alnext expert Amy Woods further exposes ongoing shop-floor woes—made visible by observing the seven wastes. But, she tells Andy, the real point is that the people doing the red-bin work *should be talking to the operators.*

## Author Comments

The deeper issue Phil is trying to get Andy to see is that organizing work for output is not enough. The challenge is to organize for learning. The basic learning method is problem-based learning: by solving detailed problems one-by-one people learn to understand their technical processes in greater depth. Getting close to one-piece-flow means tackling problems one-by-one and thus accelerating learning.

Any operational process is a system, not just a sequence of steps. Failure occurs when the weakest leak in the web fails, which is often created by unique circumstances, which is why fires keep springing out of nothing and are so hard to spot before they fully flame.

Fundamentally improving delivery can't be done just by reorganizing processes—the entire system must be improved, which needs the involvement of all and most specifically, value adding operators and their frontline managers. Andy's main problems is that he has learned to run the system with his close guard of managers, mostly technocrats themselves, but has never learned to fight at the front with the operators themselves. He has to discover from scratch how to lead from the ground up, which means creating a learning environment for production teams.

For operators to start seeing problems and coming up with suggestions, the priority is to stabilize flows to give them ownership of products, machinery and familiarity with each others in teams. This means recognizing stable value streams through the product/process matrix, stabilizing demand on the line and stabilizing teams in order to create a stable learning environment.

We see Phil's greater goal—to force Andy to own the improvement, and to do it by having operators own their own improvement. Andy needs shock therapy (practice) in order to get with the program as a real lean manager. As Amy says, "This is all about getting the line management to own their problems, and to have a daily opportunity to discuss with the staff specialists on what really goes on."

*Establish regular kaizen activities to open your eyes to the real potential for performance improvement from involving every person all the time.* Kaizen activities open your eyes to how engaged employees truly are and how your organization either involves them in working better and improving their work environment, or how focused it is on its own procedures and silo wars, heedless of value adding conditions. Kaizen activities are different from staff specialist led improvement projects, which might improve the process locally, but reinforce Taylorist thinking in the business. Kaizen activities should be led by a line manager (maybe supported by a staff expert), and the opportunity to see how responsible lien management feels for solving its own problems and how it can be helped to become more autonomous in facing and solving its own problems.

### Key Ideas

- Motion kaizen before equipment kaizen.
- Implementing motion kaizen can easily surface existing tensions rather than improve them.
- The people doing the work must be the ones improving the work. The people who spend their lives looking at and handling parts know a good deal more about what happens than you ever will.
- You need to organize problem-solving flow just like the delivery of parts. There can be no improvement without basic stability in the workplace.
- First, stabilize your value streams by having set products go through set equipment. Second, organize people so they work in fixed teams. Third, stabilize the workload so that teams build the product families at an even pace.
- The more experienced and accomplished the manager, the harder it is to realize how much they have to change their basic approach to lean leadership.

**Graphics**

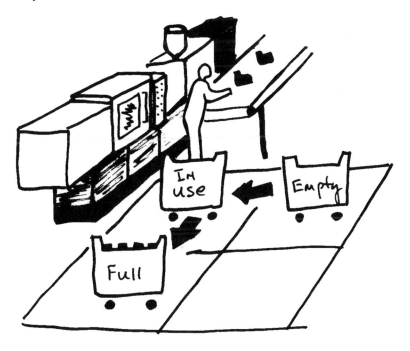

**Product Process Matrix**

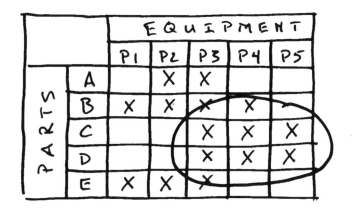

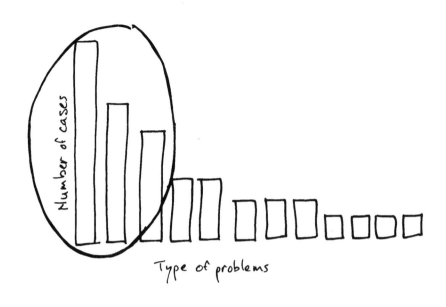

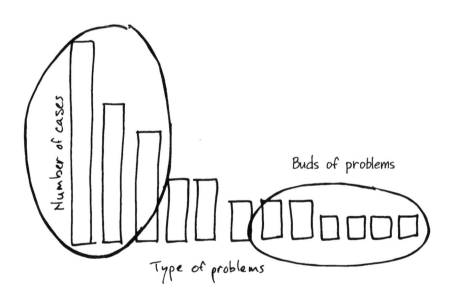

**Reflection**

What lesson(s) have you learned? Please write down your answer.

Can you think of three specific examples that illustrate this learning in your own business? Please write them down.

How are daily problems addressed by you and your team?

Who solves your problems?

What methods are used?

**Chapter 2: Answers, Notes, Questions**

*Chapter Three*

# GO AND SEE

*Fully embrace the "go and see" approach of studying the gemba to understand the capabilities, strengths, and weaknesses of your products, people and processes.*

Once again Andy finds himself with new demands from Phil, who prods him once more to practice daily genchi genbtsu (go and see for yourself to find out facts at the source to understand the true nature of the issue). He listens to Bob Woods' speech on the underlying management system of the Toyota Production System—a way to apply the behavioral values and principles that enable one to create a Buddha image without losing the ability to give it a soul as well.

Andy visits Neville's plant where he sees the impact of a manager spending the bulk of his time  on the shop floor rather than in his office. He can immediately see how a plant organized for flow appears radically different from one such as his. Simple flows are visible and easy to follow. Operators rarely leave their workstations. Instead of forklifts shuttling large pallets of components irregularly, small trains deliver materials consistently. More importantly, Andy experiences a twinge of jealously when observing Neville's strong rapport with the line operators as they tackle a problem regarding safety together.

Andy returns to his plant determined to lead kaizen through regular, ongoing PDCA. Under Phil's observation he comes to view this approach as one of experimentation designed for learning rather than something purely outcome-oriented.

## Author Comments

Gemba is a great teacher. Lean can only be learned—and taught—at the gemba and it's important to understand why. Aspects of go and see that are central to grasping lean and getting results include:

*Customer gemba*: only at the customer can you get a real grasp for what the customer is trying to do and how your product or service helps or hinders. Customers are notoriously bad at expressing "value", however, value becomes apparent when we look at what customers seek to achieve and the real-life problems they encounter, many would simply not be thought off in a meeting room.

*Encourage kaizen*: Andy's getting the point that it's all about kaizen, to get people to think and take control of their own processes. This means asking the right question. Executive role on the gemba is to fuel kaizen by showing what is a potential problem, how it reflects a larger challenge and encouraging people to work on it within their workspace. Without executive encouragement on a daily basis, kaizen first strays into solving irrelevant problems and then stops altogether.

*Sustaining kaizen*: For processes to truly improve and for this improvement to turn into results, the outcome of kaizen initiatives must be integrated in the day-to-day running of the business. This requires having the right kind of managers who can think about local kaizen and change their ways of working accordingly. Lean managers must spend time on the gemba to accompany front line managers in both the conclusions they draw from kaizen and in helping with procedural barriers to changing things, as well as constantly asking, "what next?" to keep the kaizen effort going.

*Gemba is where you develop judgment*: Fundamentally, as you spend time supporting kaizen this is where you develop a better understanding of your business challenges, where you get your teams to agree on problems and confronting rather than working around them, as well as a firsthand grasp of the strength and weaknesses of your products, services, people and processes. Thinking about these three aspects of your business is the key to see both the operational difficulties you face to grow the business, and unexpected opportunities for progress. The gemba is where you learn to align your company's efforts with what is needed to support your more successful customers and make your business succeed in their wake.

*Set up a calendar of gemba visits to open your eyes to the capabilities, strengths, and weaknesses of products, services, people, and processes.* Gemba walks are the foundational tool in lean to see for yourself, firsthand, how the reality of work conforms (or better yet, doesn't!) to theory. In a meeting room, large problems are addressed, either because the crisis is intense or because the problem is felt to be structural. Management meetings are about trying to see one's way through the fog-of-war of business in turbulent times. During a gemba walk, very detailed, specific and one-off problems will be revealed, a reflection of the friction people endure every day when they try to do good work.

Thinking at both the high level of business strategies and the detailed level of grains of sand in the processes is the key to developing a full understanding of what is really going on in your business, what the real potential and opportunities are, as well as the real-life constraints on progress and growth.

Go and see is a tool to see real people, hear their points of view and perspectives, and grasp how much work remains to do to unify them in a common understanding of the business' challenges and a common purpose, starting with their every day difficulties. Gemba walks are the most radical management tool in lean as they will change your entire perspective on how to do business and how to learn to align customer value, employee engagement and financial results.

## Key Ideas

- The role of supervisors is to create standardized work sheets with operators. These documents create basis for a simple conversation.
- Most important lean practice: going to the real place to see the real thing to learn what is really happening.
- Lean is about servicing customers better with less staff, less inventory, and less capital expenditure. You do this through managing your processes better, and with people who know what they are doing and create value, which means without the extra staff and buffers and waste of time and money.
- Toyota blends activity and results though PDCA thinking to get teams to solve problems together.
- Identify a few typical problems and drive people to solve these problems locally in greater and greater detail.
- Standardized work and kaizen are together the bedrock of TPS. Standardized work is about agreeing how the work should be done best, to better see the problems. Kaizen is about encouraging operators and frontline supervisors to solve all the problems that appear as gaps to standard.
- True aim of TPS: making everybody engaged so that everyday problem-solving turns into everyday innovation, and, in turn, more value for customers.
- True lean is not about applying lean tools to every process, but about developing a kaizen mindset in every employee.
- In a "problems first" culture managers thank employees for bringing a new problem up.
- Go and see is an opportunity for senior managers to establish direct relationships with frontline employees.
- Basic go and see unit of action is to address one problem for one operator every time you are on the shop floor.

## Graphics

**Kanban cards hung in a neat queue**

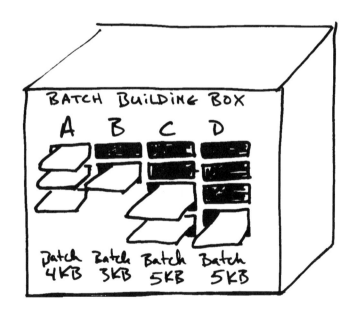

## TRACKING OF PRODUCTION

| 6:00 | Production | Programmed stops | change-overs | Organization problems | Break-downs | Remarks |
|---|---|---|---|---|---|---|
| 6:30 | | | | | | |
| 7:00 | | | | | | |
| 7:30 | | | | | | |
| 8:00 | | | | | | |
| etc. | | | | | | etc. |
| 12:00 | | | | | | |
| 12:30 | | | | | | |
| 1:00 | | | | | | |
| 1:30 | | | | | | |
| 2:00 TOTAL | | | | | | |

| Part # | Standard Cycle Time | | # of Good Parts | Productive Time | |
|---|---|---|---|---|---|
| | | X | | | + |
| | | X | | = | + |
| | | X | | = | + |
| | | | TOTAL | | |
| | | | OEU | | |

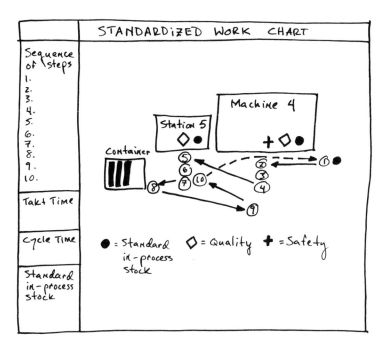

### Reflection

What lesson(s) have you learned? Please write down your answer.

Can you think of three specific examples that illustrate this learning in your own business? Please write them down.

What do you observe at your gemba?

What have you learned from careful observation of your work, your customer hand off, your processes?

# Chapter 3: Answers, Notes, Questions

*Chapter Four*

# MANAGING MEANS IMPROVING

*Reveal and share problems through visual management to help people frame challenges as manageable gaps between planned and actual.*

Bob Woods pays a to visit Vaudon. A lean manager's job is to create an environment where problems can be solved by the people working in the process themselves. On the shop floor, Woods and Phil challenge Andy and his workers on how well they are organized as a clear flow of problem-solving, clarifying ways to break down, prioritize, and address gaps as a team. At one point Andy loses his temper with his team, frustrated at their resistance and defensiveness at this new approach.

Later at dinner at his home, Andy asks how this small-step improvement approach actually translates into dramatic business savings (which Phil continues to demand). How does eliminating waste in the manufacturing process dramatically boost profits and create opportunities? He also wonders how improvements in the plant can be reconciled with ingrained suspicion that jobs will be cut.

Andy realizes that he has been spending a lot more time on the floor, participating in red-bin reviews, leading discussions on jidoka, and moving forward with heretofore heated arguments by rooting them in a more rigorous exploration of the detailed facts. Woods and Phil note his progress (especially his growing technical know-how), push him to continue practicing PDCA, and hold out hope for the Vaudon plant.

## Author Comments

To work well you have to work better—kaizen is essential to superior performance. Without constant kaizen, processes will run into problems and deteriorate. Kaizen keeps both processes working and managers honest.

To spur kaizen, people have to be taught to see the improvement potential in their routine work. The way to do this is to get them to plan their day, measure their performance, and then ask themselves how can they improve their work every day. Once people begin to seek improvement, they will need help with spotting opportunities. Visual management is necessary to structure the workplace to reveal problems. This is mostly done with the use of standards and by teaching people to distinguish between normal and abnormal situations. Managers must become teachers. To successfully become lean they must teach:

- Work, and steer people to a deeper understanding of the technical knowledge underlying their job—Woods sees hope in Andy when the latter finally shows an interest in injection pressing rather than stay focused at the procedural level.

- Improvement to keep teams at their best by engaging them in exchanging improvement ideas amongst themselves and encouraging them to investigate issues beyond organizational boundaries to deepen both their understanding and teamwork across departments.

*Learn to visualize planned vs. actual to open your eyes to how people interpret the causes of the obstacles stopping them from performing better.* The lean tradition is rich in techniques to visualize processes in order to reveal problems. Visualizing processes is often simple but not easy. Managers often resist revealing problems to both senior management and workers. The quality and discipline in maintaining visual tools reflects on the determination of the managers to tackle one problem at a time in order to improve their department's practices.

## Key Points

- Producing people before producing parts means getting everybody to solve problems every day—solving problems starts when people are able to recognize problems. And management's role is to support this with visual controls and other methods.
- Problem-solving requires constant vigilance in the face of forces such as overproduction (which hides problems).
- The productive way to frame a problem is as a gap to standard.
- Kaizen is not a separate or isolated activity atop one's work; it is the mainstay of everyone's (especially the manager's) daily work.
- Pull gives an architecture to kaizen.
- One must always apply lean tools rigorously as an "in" into a problem; the tools frame problems in a lean way. They don't provide answers per se; but enable teams to frame issues so that they make conduct productive experiments.
- The Check and Act part of the PDCA cycle require a radical transformation of managerial behavior—learning to draw the right conclusions from the experiment takes practice, and requires that one knows what one is checking in the first place.
- Moreover, this must be framed as *learning*—what did we learn, and what conclusions can we draw from the experiment?
- The long-term practice of manager-worker PDCA produces a new form of organizational knowledge (and "culture") that ultimately becomes a form of competitive advantage that is virtually unbeatable.
- The lean revolution is about teaching line management to solve its own context-specific problems through visualization and problem-solving.

### Reflection

What lesson(s) have you learned? Please write down your answer.

Can you think of three specific examples that illustrate this learning in your own business? Please write them down.

What level of managerial support is most helpful to you?

What do you need from your managers to learn and practice effective problem-solving?

Who ties your kaizen work to business results?

### Chapter 4: Answers, Notes, Questions

*Chapter Five*

# CLEAR DIRECTION

*Establish and share a list of key performance indicators linking value-creating work with business performance.*

At the plant, Andy discovers that while the kaizen work has improved operations, many operators continue to harbor suspicions that Phil's agenda is to make it look nice so that he extract more profits and then either close or sell the plant. Phil continues to push him, preparing for product transfers to the Polish plant, asking him to implement a pull system.

Phil asks Andy to assess all the real costs of making products in his plant, and to start seeing them systematically. So-called point optimization strategies tend to reduce costs in one area—only to create larger problems elsewhere, he says. What's needed are shared purpose and shared indicators of success so that people see not only their own improvements; but how these tie into the bigger stream.

Now that Andy has taken to problem-solving with passion, Phil says he must learn with his team to clarify the most important problems to address. They do so together by establishing numerical indicators linked to Nexplas budgets that create a bridge between financial performance and shop-floor improvements.

Amy visits the Vaudon plant and immediately tells Andy that a pull system is in fact linked to clear direction—by helping move the right problems forward towards resolution. "You need both the tool—the *what*—and the method—the *how*." Later on, Andy learns at the company's meeting that his plant is not on the chopping block.

## Author Comments

Man, by nature is a political animal—no matter how inconvenient this often turns out to be. Business issues are both technical and political, and there is no avoiding the political side of things. Having confidence in fair leaders that know what they're doing is essential to people's morale, which, in turn, is essential to achieving results.

Supporting a lot of kaizen is a great way to develop people, but it can also add confusion if it pushes many changes in many places. A clear direction is essential to retain people's confidence. This means translating business issues into performance indicators so that every one understands what success is in operational terms.

Having a set of ten to twelve key performance indicators clearly establishes where progress is expected. In addition to these indicators, clarifying the main challenges and the overall kaizen strategy for each also helps to make sure people understand what you're trying to do.

Complete customer satisfaction is a sensible business objective. Trying to do this by visiting the gemba for every complaint is a reasonable way to start. Employees might not believe the effectiveness of the proposed measure, but they will understand what you're trying to achieve. A key to defining clear direction is to list the principal challenges and planned responses.

Clear direction also helps at corporate level because you can rally the thoughtful people to your ideas by putting them across clearly— meaning is often an essential part of trust.

*Establish a shortlist of key performance indicators to open your eyes to how business level performance challenges translate at the value-creating level.* A main point of asking lean questions—such as how to better satisfy customers? how to reduce lead-time? how to stop closer to defects? how to encourage people to improve their work methods to reach better standardized work?—is that they will make you discover your real business challenges.

Creating a clear set of performance indicators and improvement targets defines goals for dynamic success. Spelling out the challenges defines the improvement direction. By practicing these tools you can test how clear you are on:

1) the challenges for the business you want to share with all employees,

2) the improvement method to face these challenges, and

3) the progress objectives set on key indicators to see how quickly goals are achieved or where we collectively go down the wrong path because we've not clearly understood what the challenge really is.

### Key Ideas

- While kaizen improvements are the basis of lean work, they must be tied to business results through the use of clear direction. Any work site is a closed system in which gains in one area invariably cause waste elsewhere.
- Going to the gemba is not enough on its own. You need to establish a clear direction and make sure efforts are concentrated on high-payoff problems.
- Activities are key to learning, but results the only proof of learning. It's about learning to find the right activities to get the right results.
- Use lean to define reality through typical problems, which have typical solutions.
- North Star targets should define the essential dimensions of desired improvement—the pace of progress—without being too limited. They are clear ways mark progress without an endpoint.
- These targets start with budget objectives, which then establish the operational improvements (reduction in defects, improvement in productivity, reduction in stock, etc) needed to achieve them.

## Graphics

### Display board for truck packing

| Truck destination | Departure time | Preparation zone | Start of preparation time | End of preparation time | Status | Comments |
|---|---|---|---|---|---|---|
| | | | | | | |
| | | | | | | |
| | | | | | | |
| | | | | | | |

### Load leveling box for Line 1

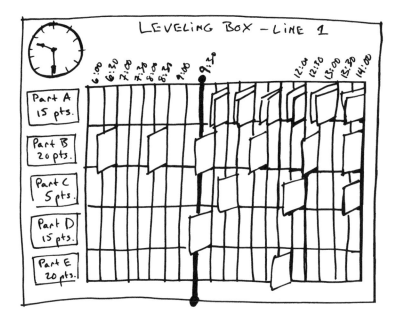

## "Go and See" on the production line

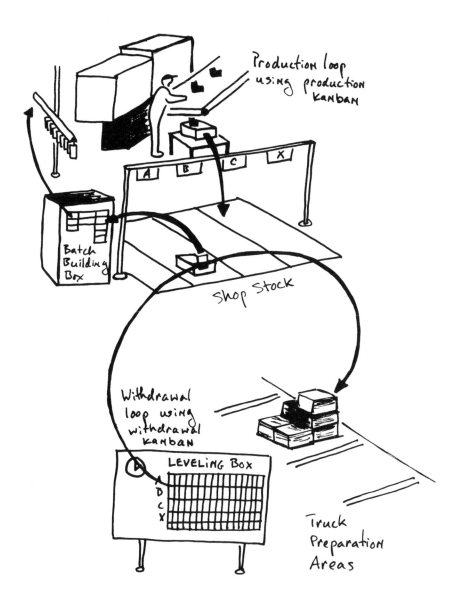

**Andy Ward's North Star**

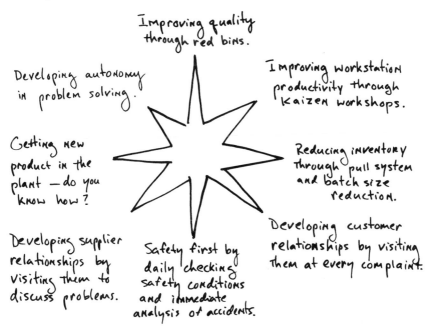

Improving quality through red bins.

Developing autonomy in problem solving.

Improving workstation productivity through Kaizen workshops.

Getting new product in the plant — do you know how?

Reducing inventory through pull system and batch size reduction.

Developing supplier relationships by visiting them to discuss problems.

Safety first by daily checking safety conditions and immediate analysis of accidents.

Developing customer relationships by visiting them at every complaint.

## Reflection

What lesson(s) have you learned? Please write down your answer (*see page 78*).

Can you think of three specific examples that illustrate this learning in your own business? Please write them down.

What is your True North?

What indicators take you there?

How do you determine these metrics?

# Chapter 5: Answers, Notes, Questions

# Chapter Six

# TEAMWORK

*Establish weekly team meetings to gauge how well you are leveling production, reveal the amount of rework, and boost teamwork through a regular cadence of shared problem-solving.*

Andy Ward challenges his workers to build on their lean progress. With Muller as production manager, teams have stepped up their problem-solving activities. Andy continues to support this at the floor by helping provide direction, clarifying problems, and engaging at a detailed level. Yet when he confesses to Jenkinson that deploying the pull system has in fact destabilized work as much as strengthened it, Phil suggests that Andy's major challenge now is fostering teamwork.

Specifically, the pull system has reduced stocks yet also lowered on-time delivery, which happens when you have pulling without leveling. This underlies the current challenge: to level, you need actual teamwork, which translates operationally into having all teams get together weekly to produce a leveled production plan.

Andy realizes that having these meetings on a weekly cadence builds teamwork and that teamwork is not a matter of people getting along but of them *solving difficult problems together*. He learns how to use an A3 form as a way of structuring a common approach to problem solving and creating teamwork.

As the plant more deeply implements a pull system with leveling of demand, visualization of problems production analysis boards, and A3 thinking, Andy shares with Phil that they may have hit a plateau. Increased productivity has eliminated the use of temps and he can no longer take people out of work without making them redundant.

### Author Comments

Teamwork is an individual skill. This is another counterintuitive insight of lean. Practicing respect means seeking to reach your goals by developing people. Developing people means, of course, deepening their technical ability, but it also means developing their ability to work with colleagues across boundaries.

The most effective people in any organization are those who are both technically competent and thoroughly connected. Both skills are necessary. Developing teamwork is a matter of developing more people who can easily work with others, upstream and downstream.

The lean way of doing so is by cross-functional problem solving and improvement activities. The ability to work together grows from deepening collaboration, but also by taking into account a person's background and experience, and learning to listen in terms different from your own. Understanding doesn't mean agreement—yet. Understanding is more than either information or knowledge, it's what makes the business work at all levels.

*Learn to organize a weekly production meeting to set next week's level plan, to open your eyes to all the rework due to mishandled mishaps.* The weekly production planning meeting's ultimate goal is teamwork. The immediate aim of the meeting is producing a leveled plan per part: customer demand is averaged to come up with a stable number for at least a week, two if possible, and forecast numbers are run to generate an estimate of the following ten weeks. Each participant in the meeting is asked what special effort or needs they have to achieve the plans. If there is a problem, the cross-functional team works together to come up with a plan in order to deliver the leveled production.

The weekly production meeting is essentially an exercise in teamwork: rather than just solving issues within their own silos, functional heads have to agree to work on problems together. They learn to collaborate better, and to better coordinate, so that just-in-time can be further tightened and progress continued.

## Key Points

- Successfully implementing a pull system entails the human challenge of fostering teamwork just as it calls for understanding and mastery of the mechanics of the method.
- Production copes with production-caused variation, and logistics with customer-caused variation.
- The first principle of pull is always to have the right stock at the right place.
- Real teamwork is cooperation across boundaries, extending beyond functions.
- People learn to work together by solving problems together.
- Lean theory of learning: 1) You learn by doing. 2) You learn better in a team. 3) Teams learn when they try to solve problems together.
- Flow operates at two basic levels: parts and knowledge. Learn about improving the flow of good parts at a lower cost and improving the knowledge flow of good ideas by involving and developing people.

## Graphics

### Customer demand for Vaudon products

| | Week 31: Demand 700 | | | | | | | Week 32: Demand 700 | | | | | | | Week 33: Demand 680 | | | | | |
|---|---|---|---|---|---|---|---|---|---|---|---|---|---|---|---|---|---|---|---|---|
| | M | T | W | T | F | S | S | M | T | W | T | F | S | S | M | T | W | T | F | |
| Customer demand | 150 | 160 | 140 | 20 | 90 | 140 | 0 | 170 | 180 | 140 | 110 | 120 | 0 | 0 | 150 | 90 | 120 | 140 | 180 | 110.5 |
| Production | 160 | 120 | 150 | 160 | 140 | 0 | 0 | 110 | 140 | 170 | 180 | 140 | 0 | 0 | 110 | 120 | 150 | 90 | 120 | |
| Stock | 200 | 160 | 170 | 310 | 360 | 220 | 220 | 160 | 120 | 150 | 220 | 240 | 240 | 240 | 200 | 230 | 260 | 210 | 150 | 213.7 |

## Takt time applied to customer demand for Vaudon products

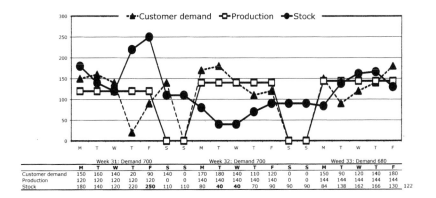

| | Week 31: Demand 700 | | | | | | | Week 32: Demand 700 | | | | | | | Weed 33: Demand 680 | | | | | |
|---|---|---|---|---|---|---|---|---|---|---|---|---|---|---|---|---|---|---|---|---|
| | **M** | **T** | **W** | **T** | **F** | **S** | **S** | **M** | **T** | **W** | **T** | **F** | **S** | **S** | **M** | **T** | **W** | **T** | **F** | |
| Customer demand | 150 | 160 | 140 | 20 | 90 | 140 | 0 | 170 | 180 | 140 | 110 | 120 | 0 | 0 | 150 | 90 | 120 | 140 | 180 | |
| Production | 120 | 120 | 120 | 120 | 120 | 0 | 0 | 140 | 140 | 140 | 140 | 140 | 0 | 0 | 144 | 144 | 144 | 144 | 144 | |
| Stock | 180 | 140 | 120 | 220 | **250** | 110 | 110 | 80 | **40** | **40** | 70 | 90 | 90 | 90 | 84 | 138 | 162 | 166 | 130 | 122 |

## Fixed-quantity, fixed-time leveling with kanban

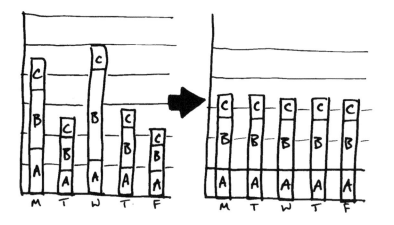

**2-year capacity life-cycle plan**

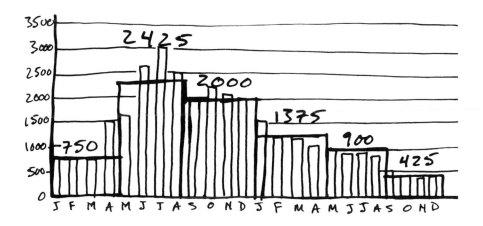

**Group problem solving and information sharing diagrams**

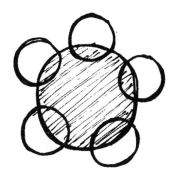 

**A3 outline**

| Title | DATE | Supervisor | Owner |
|---|---|---|---|
| Problem description | Root-cause analysis | | |
| Grasp the situation | Countermeasure plan | | |
| | Execution plan | | |
| | Checking results | | |
| Target | Followup and learning points | | |

**Reflection**

What lesson(s) have you learned? Please write down your answer.

Can you think of three specific examples that illustrate this learning in your own business? Please write them down.

How does problem-solving tie into teamwork for you?

Do you have a way of "framing" problems that in fact invites people to share data and understand purpose better?

Does your workplace value right over being curious?

# Chapter 6: Answers, Notes, Questions

*Chapter Seven*

# MUTUAL TRUST

*Use A3 thinking as a way of combating silo thinking by gaining agreement on the problem definition and aligning all individuals around a common goal.*

While visiting a Czech factory that has chosen another approach to Phil Jenkinson's demands (focusing narrowly on reducing batch sizes and controlling changeovers), Andy Ward hears distressing news: his workers have gone on strike. He immediately contacts Phil, who pledges to support Andy conditionally. The plant no longer has the Czech work; and if any customers are lost due to the strike he will shut the plant down. He will however keep corporate away so that Andy can get to the root cause of the dispute and deal with it.

Andy confronts his striking workers in the company cafeteria. Dropping his guard, he shares with everyone that while their suspicions that Phil wanted to close the plant were true a year ago, Andy has in fact fought successfully to turn this around—a position now jeopardized by the strike. He agrees to a short-term demand that workers will not be required to stand at their stations, as well as an agreement to hear their full concerns. Upon resumption of work, Andy probes deeper into the root cause of this breakdown.

He concludes that for this system to work, mutual trust must be the bedrock foundation of successful team efforts and problem solving. "It's not about sides, it's about working together." Moreover, he cannot simply state this as policy. His job as manager—as leader— is to live these ideals daily, and that the hardest challenge for him is recognizing how much *he* must continue to change his beliefs and ways of thinking.

## Author Comments

Confidence has an economic value, a fact well-known to economists, no matter how many managers refuse to accept it. To work well, people need to be confident, first in their skills, second in the competence of their managers, third that there is a collective future in which they have a future and fourth that they will be treated fairly by the organization as a whole. Barring any of these elements, morale is low, and so is customer focus and productivity.

In lean thinking, mutual trust is grounded on the mutual ownership of problems, which means developing the discipline of listening to problems first and of accepting negative information with curiosity and open mindedness rather than by shooting the messenger. Negative people can be abrasive, but they're not necessarily wrong. Developing this discipline in managers rests on 1) going to the workplace to see for oneself and listen to the voice of employees, 2) ask "why?" repeatedly to make sure the ins and outs of any situation are shared and understood, 3) paying earnest regard to unfavorable information. Problems first.

Mutual trust is achieved by aligning employee satisfaction and pride in their work and the company with the business' success in contributing to society. This means a commitment from leaders to stabilize employment conditions and offer development possibilities to every person according to their full abilities, and energizing employees so that they contribute actively to the success of the company, not just by creating value through their work but by adding value through their ideas.

*Use A3 as a tool to gain agreement on the problem definition—to open your eyes to see how much silo thinking interprets everything solipsisticly instead of as part of a larger whole.* A3 is not just about solving problems—it's a process to develop teamwork and trust. As the A3 is being written, the author passes it on to key stakeholders to garner their views. Not every one can be pleased by the conclusion, but every one concerned can be consulted. Then, the completed A3 is presented to the rest of the management team. The aim of such presentations is to:

1) Engage people in thinking more deeply about the issues by supporting a discussion.

2) Develop self-confidence in the authors by letting them see for themselves that they can solve issues—not all change is impossible and they can have an impact about how things are done

3) Develop mutual trust as the management team members see that each of them is trying hard to improve things and that, collectively they can reach across their functional boundaries and trust their colleagues to give them a hand to resolve cross-functional issues.


### Key Points

• You can't force change without creating push back.
• Every lean tool can be used either to develop mutual trust and smarter work or to extract greater productivity, fewer jobs, and less trust.
• These two approaches are choices between treating people as slaves to the machine or as individuals who are in control of the process.
• Only people can improve their own processes.
• Mutual trust is a tool and technique as well as a basic principle. Core is that people feel you take their problems seriously.
• Very long to grow; and needs to be reinforced continuously.
• Without mutual trust everything (go see, kaizen, clear direction, and teamwork) is bound to fail.

## Reflection

What lesson(s) have you learned? Please write down your answer.

Can you think of three specific examples that illustrate this learning in your own business? Please write them down.

Where does the value of trust produce tangible benefits at your workplace?

What practices does trust enable for you and your team?

## Chapter 7: Answers, Notes, Questions

# Chapter Eight

# CREATING VALUE

*Solicit and act upon employee suggestions in a way that tests each one and pulls further input and improvement.*

Andy Ward experiences a familiar feeling of self-doubt during the successful implementation of a plant-wide suggestion system when an operator's recommendation for improving a jig reveals his own technical limitations once more. Nonetheless he thanks her for this; and then thanks her again when she volunteers that she and others would like to come over the weekend to paint the plant in advance of an important visit by a new potential client.

Assessing the current state of the plant to gauge its appeal to the potential client, Phil commends Andy for his visual board displaying metrics for operating, changeover, lot loaded, breakdown, as a means of revealing if and where the plant has free capacity.

Phil's assurance of Andy's progress leads the manager to share his newest problem: his manufacturing manager Bayard, having taken to kaizen work with a passion, has become so passionate about the specs for a new part that he has begun arguing about both the design and the planned production process with the engineers.

In the spirit of lean, Andy begins to consider how to structure experiments so that he can develop kaizen spirit in his engineers. As *improvement after improvement* becomes the normal way of working in his plant, he listens to yet another lecture from his boss to always practice go and see.

"Ultimately, that's what distinguishes those who 'get it' from those who don't," says Phil, "It all happens at the gemba."

## Author Comments

Ultimately, a company is its products or services. Customers use the products they buy to perform a service. They expect from the service they get that it solves a problem. The business' ability to prosper rests on its technical capability to improve products and services by better understanding the link between improving products currently in production and better designing future products.

The real scope of kaizen goes far beyond improving local productivity—the true aim is improving products and services to customers. This requires building the teamwork necessary to translate improvement ideas into engineering changes. This is the ultimate goal of the lean approach of "good thinking, good products," and it needs to be carefully steered and nurtured by the company's leaders.

The leader is the one person who can see the whole picture and establish the link between how customers use products and services to support their lifestyles, how this usage could be improved right now in current products and services, and how this learning can be translated into the design of the next generation of products and services. This skill is the holy grail of lean.

*Nurture employee suggestions to open your eyes to the power of sustaining a flow of improvement ideas in the business.* Employee suggestions are the real aim of the entire lean system, which acts as a scaffolding to create space for people to think and share their ideas. Obtaining suggestions is a key managerial skill, which starts with asking the right question, then helping people formulate their ideas (don't reformulate—they'll feel you're stealing their idea!), then find the place and space to test this idea in simple, not costly ways. If the idea pans out, the next step is to convince other employees or other department to adopt it, and finally the department procedures themselves must be change.

Suggestions create a bridge between individual intelligence and collective intelligence, and this can be rewarded by recognizing the "suggestion of the month." Suggestions are essentially a test of managerial attitude to learning. Some managers will know how to encourage suggestions, support them and then change their own ways of working accordingly. Others will be curious about suggestions, but never actually make the step of improving their own procedures accordingly. Others yet will try to appropriate themselves the idea. Watching how suggestions are handled gives you a great insight into what kind of organization you want to create and scale-up.

### Key Points

- Value analysis leads to value engineering.
- Kaizen spirit has an even greater impact at the engineering phase than in actual production.
- Red bins, pull system, and kaizen workshops reveal individual's understanding of the product; which leads to greater awareness of how company builds and designs the parts. Which ultimately enables greater customer value.
- The ultimate goal of lean is to deliver better products to the market.
- Making people before making parts means developing more knowledgeable people who will design better products than the competition from the customers' point-of-view and with leaner processes that the competition can't match cost-wise.
- This systems approach highlights lean as a source of sustainable competitive advantage.

## Reflection

What lesson(s) have you learned? Please write down your answer.

Can you think of three specific examples that illustrate this learning in your own business? Please write them down.

What are you learning about your product/service from your experiments?

What ideas do you have for improving your product/service?

## Chapter 8: Notes, Questions, Answers

# LEAD WITH RESPECT

Our core belief is achieving our objectives through developing our people. Lead with respect is a practice, mind you—a number of actions and approaches that enable us to realize this as something we do, rather than as something we merely say.

–Andrew Ward

# Chapter One

# LEAD FROM THE GROUND UP

*Lead lean by challenging your teams on the gemba to see and close the gaps between ideal/planned and actual.*

Jane Delaney can barely contain her anger when her key client's VP Andy Ward sums up the source of their current problem—*her*. Southcape Software has been missing deadlines and failing to deliver the key elements of their software for this automotive supplier; yet Andy chastises Jane personally. As the company's senior executive, he says it's her job to make sure her people succeed. "They have a right to succeed, not an obligation," he says.

Andy explains that Nexplas operates on a core belief of achieving its business objectives through developing its people. This lead with respect is a daily practice comprised of specific actions and approaches. Andy offers to teach Jane this different approach to work—if she is willing to learn.

Jane shares the current state with her management team. They blame the current delivery breakdowns on their client. Jane hears this, yet responds to by saying that Southcape will do exactly what Nexplas has demanded in order to keep the business.

Jane calls Andy and agrees to take him at his word—to learn the model and work to preserve their work relationship. Lead with respect starts with "go and see," going to the place where work happens and finding the facts directly by yourself at the source. Andy invites Jane to come visit his production factory in Swindon to observe.

## Author Comments

Lean leadership can be learned—and taught. However, leaders must first come to terms with the fact that their results, regardless of the environment, are a reflection of how they lead. To learn lean leadership, a leader first needs to accept that they need to learn.

Lean leadership is different from any other leadership styles inasmuch as it doesn't rest on innate traits, such as charisma, vision, belief in yourself and so forth. Lean leadership centers on first a commitment to develop yourself, and then to develop others. Developing others means finding a balance between challenging and listening, teaching and supporting, encouraging teamwork and learning from what teams suggest.

The first step, is taking responsibility for your department's results and committing to seeking superior performance through the development of your people. This can only happen on the gemba, with customers, at the workplace, at suppliers, anywhere where work actually happens. Lean leadership starts from the ground up.

*Challenge your teams on the gemba to open your eyes to the gap between outcomes and outputs.* Challenging teams and managers is a key lean tool. We seek dynamic progress, not static optimization. Yet, not surprisingly, most people will show you how they've tried to optimize their process without challenging the waste the process really generates. A typical example would be trying to reduce the number of steps an operator makes to improve productivity without first tackling all the rework and rejects created out of not achieving right first time. To challenge others you must learn to:

- Stand in the circle and mentally force yourself to see what could be the ideal one-piece-flow quality instantaneous delivery to the customer, one by one in sequence with 100% value added.
- Think hard, observe and come up with possible countermeasures you then do not share.

- Challenge teams on their objectives and potential counter-measure areas to get them thinking without ever giving them specific solutions.
- Support them as they try something, even if it seems wrong to you at first, and follow their progress.
- Ask yourself what you have learned, and identify people who show promise in coming up with ingenious, low-cost ideas and the ability to make them work, in order to further develop them and promote them.

### Key Points

- Lean is not about pushing or exploiting people; quite the opposite.
- Lean practice pushes people to work better and smarter while providing the support and coaching to enable this to actually happen.
- Lean is about challenging yourself and others to find the right problems and working hard every day to engage people in solving them.
- Lean = kaizen + respect.
- Lean and respect are about people but not in a "soft" sentimental manner: to improve processes you must improve the individual competencies and teamwork ability of your people.
- Once your people are better at what they do than others, your processes cannot be copied by your competitors—a superior competitive advantage since others can't follow the same learning curve.
- Sustainable results can be achieved only within stable relationships based on mutual trust.

## Graphics

### Seven Practices of Lead with Respect

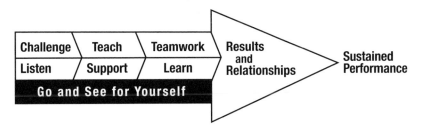

### Reflection

What lesson(s) have you learned? Please write down your answer (*see page 100*).

Can you think of three specific examples that illustrate this learning in your own business? Please write them down.

What does lean mean to you?

What does respect mean to you?

Can one actually "practice" respect, and if so, what behaviors does this show up as in daily work?

# Chapter 1: Answers, Notes, Questions

*Chapter Two*

# ALIGN SUCCESS WITH VALUE

*Visualize customer problems to reveal how much focus is on internal processes rather than customer delivery.*

Jane initially struggles with the idea of relating lean practice on a loud factory floor to her company's software work, especially when, for instance, there are no forklifts to avoid in her air-conditioned cubicles. "The key to satisfied customers is satisfied employees," Andy counters, explaining that lean practice always starts with safety concerns in every setting.

Andy's primary responsibility (like Jane) is to create a system that enables people to succeed, he says; the first step (after safety) is leading employees on aligning their personal success on delivering value to customers. Most workplaces track the wrong metrics of success because they have no bearing on customer value.

Together they work with operators who share the purpose of a logistics whiteboard and a logistics tracking chart: to improve delivery of products to customers by identifying manageable goals that lead to improved success. Andy says that coupling these measures with daily kaizen (small step success) forms the basis of their strategic approach.

Jane accepts his message that people come to work to make good parts (and write good code) and returns to Southcape with the goal of better understanding individual's problems, and to link their work with business success. She manages to convince her team to adapt a small-step approach to improvement, for starters, and enlists their support in defining success for every one of their projects.

## Author Comments

What is a successful day? Ask this question anywhere and you'll most likely get confusion. Most organizations prescribes what needs to be done, but don't say much about what success looks like. The focus is on output, rarely outcomes. Understanding success, however, is what people need in order to succeed—you find what you look for.

Aligning success with value means discussing at the workplace how achieving targets relates to customer satisfaction. The by visualizing the plan and what keeps us from achieving the plan we can build together an understanding of how we contribute to customers through our work, how we don't deliver full value because of barriers and obstacles, and so how we can improve the value through kaizen. Bridging the link between customer value and daily work is what gives meaning to work.

To develop your lean leadership, take a step back in any situation on the gemba and ask yourself: how is success being defined here. If it isn't, how to people interpret success locally? How does this align with customer value?

*Visualize customer delivery with a whiteboard to see how much the organization is internally focused on its own processes and how little on real customer service.* Astonishingly, the customer delivery board remains one of the most difficult tools to implement: which customer, when do we deliver, when is the work ready in advance, where can we find the work, what is the current status, what comments do people have regards to obstacles they encounter? Visualizing customer delivery is a key, early tool that often reveals how the status quo is going to fight progress. Bringing the customer into the processes to focus on delivery and give meaning to work is step one, yet often a surprisingly difficult one: don't skip it, don't work around it. Face the problem and align team success with customer delivery, good work, on time, in full.

## Key Points

- People have a right to succeed.
- Workers must align their personal success with the value that customers expect.
- Motivation comes from success, not the other way around (i.e., when people feel successful in their job, they're motivated to come to work and give it their best.)
- One set of activities to lead with respect: 1) learn to see your problems, 2) follow your customers, 3) accelerate your flows, 4) develop your people, 5) be very good at a few things, 6) develop long-term partnerships.
- Getting lean right involves recognizing where and how the pieces of the system fit together. For example, accelerating flows is no more than a technique for getting problems to emerge. Moreover, accelerating flows can be a "compass for improvement" that steers attention to problems that might otherwise be ignored.

## Graphics

### Logistics whiteboard

| Truck (client) | Depart date | Depart time | Prep zone | End of prep time | Status | Comments |
|---|---|---|---|---|---|---|
|  |  |  |  |  |  |  |
|  |  |  |  |  |  |  |
|  |  |  |  |  |  |  |
|  |  |  |  |  |  |  |
|  |  |  |  |  |  |  |

## Logistics tracking chart

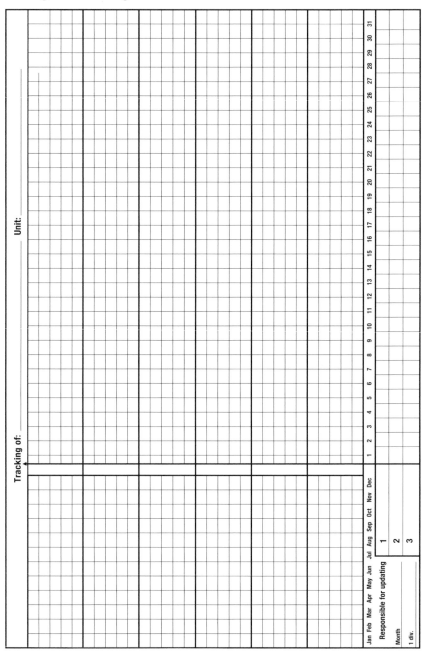

**Production Target Board**

| HOUR | TARGET | ACTUAL | COMMENTS |
|------|--------|--------|----------|
| 1 | 68 | 56 | |
| 2 | 68 | 67 | |
| 3 | 68 | 65 | |
| 4 | 68 | 59 | |
| 5 | 68 | | |
| 6 | 68 | | |
| 7 | 68 | | |
| 8 | 68 | | |

**Core Activities**

## Go and see and face your problems

**SALES**
Follow your customers

**CASH**
Accelerate your flows

**PROFIT**
Develop your people

**CAP EX**
Be very good at a few things

## Develop long-term partnerships

### Reflection

What lesson(s) have you learned? Please write down your answer.

Can you think of three specific examples that illustrate this learning in your own business? Please write them down.

What are your measures of success?

How are they gauged, tracked, reported on?

What is done with them?

Who creates and checks on the status of these numbers?

What is a successful day for you?

### Chapter 2: Answers, Notes, Questions

*Chapter Three*

# MANAGING BY PROBLEM SOLVING

*Engage employees in their own self-development by establishing problem-solving boards and a team structure for learning.*

Jane applies Andy's advice by defining success through helping people focus on rework, re-releases, and customer lead time; working closely with her managers to see how these numbers eventually effect project release dates and in fact profitability. She shares her frustration with Andy that the more she investigates their work in details, the more mess she turns up. Which Andy hears as good news.

*Problems first*, he tells Jane, is the basic attitude underlying the success of Nexplas' lean management approach. Yet when she takes this to Southcape, posting project plans on the walls and engaging more directly with workers, she becomes frustrated by the vagueness of most project managers about product definitions and current status. Being aware of problems has not improved work; in fact she feels it has does the opposite.

Andy draws a wall chart structuring an approach where both manager and worker do shared analysis of a problem and a plan to address it. They spend time with a programmer working to hear his problem, and then dig to get to the root cause of it. Andy rejects the first solution of replacing the slow computer (first course is to attack problems without investment) and helps form a new countermeasure.

After talking with the operators at Andy's plant, Jane learns the importance of a system that spots defects immediately (red bins at this plant, auto-testing for her coders). She takes this insight back to her team, asking for Southcape to build teamwork by applying this problems first approach to cross-functional difficulties.

## Author Comments

Adults don't learn the same way that young people do, which is why classroom teaching can be effective with kids but gets very poor results for adults. Adults learn by integrating their experience with new facts. Also, adults learn within a teacher-learner collaboration more than in a classroom situation. Consequently, one-to-one problem-based learning is the most effective method to teach adults as opposed to one-to-many classroom lecturing.

To learn, an adult has to solve the entire problem by themselves, and then discuss their conclusions with their teacher and/or colleagues. To facilitate these exchanges, lean breaks down problems into 1) problem, 2) cause, 3) countermeasure, 4) check status.

To develop as a leader, you need to take time to ask people to solve daily performance problems and then, with respect for their experience, discuss how they solved it until their thinking is clear. Focusing on daily problem solving, one by one and one on one is the key to engaging people in their own learning, as well as deepening your own understanding of the situation and their capabilities. Don't solve problems for people, teach them how to solve their own problems, so that they learn about their own jobs. In sharing meaningful experiences and supporting countermeasures (even when these fail) you nurture a bond of trust through facing difficulties together.

*Learn to set up problem-solving boards to open your eyes to the need to engage employees in their own self-development.* The problem list (date, problem, cause, countermeasure, check) is a tool for people to explicitly show their way of thinking about situations so it can be shared and discussed, and so that they can learn. Adults can't escape their own experience and know what they know (or think they do). Discussing their thinking about how they solved a problem and what conclusions they reached is a way to get them to reflect on their own experience and reasoning, and to learn through their experience.

## Key Points

- Lead with respect is tied to the ability and willingness of managers and workers to face problems.
- While surfacing problems is essential, it is neither easy nor comfortable—and will in all likelihood escalate tensions initially rather than diffuse them.
- Teamwork is a skill: learning to solve problems across boundaries.
- Leader's role sometime is merely asking why: managing by problem-solving is not about solving every problem but building better relationships between workers and managers so that they can solve their own problems.
- Asking why is about seeking the root cause of the problem collaboratively.
- It's all about why and not who. Asking why habitually breaks through instinctual barriers of blame and fault, enabling shared thinking—the first step to teamwork.
- It's awkward!

## Graphics

### Status Board

| Date | Problem | Cause | Countermeasure | Who does it concern | Status |
|------|---------|-------|----------------|---------------------|--------|
|      |         |       |                |                     |        |
|      |         |       |                |                     |        |
|      |         |       |                |                     |        |
|      |         |       |                |                     |        |

**Reflection**

What lesson(s) have you learned? Please write down your answer. Can you think of three specific examples that illustrate this learning in your own business? Please write them down.

Why? Why? Why? Why? Why?

**Chapter 3: Answers, Notes, Questions**

*Chapter Four*

# INVOLVE EVERYONE IN IMPROVEMENT

*Develop every person individually through creating personal plans and conducting regular reviews.*

Jane catches up with her company's tech star, Mike Wembley, who has returned to help her implement lean. As a first step he has helped create a simple andon light that indicates the moment when there's a crash in the code—baby steps towards identifying problems as they crop up in real time.

Later Jane complains to Andy that while Southcape's new internal emphasis on improving through problem-solving has helped regain two big clients they thought they'd lost, she still feels that too few things are being fixed. Andy counters that this new approach is helping her company create better relationships with its workers *and* its customers. He points out that expecting to speed things up without first reducing variation is simply copying Toyota's "best practices" without actually learning the sustainable lesson: it's a capability issue, not a process one. He says, "If we design clever processes for people and machines that don't have the capability to deal with what's thrown at them, the result will be even more chaos than before."

The lean approach is: great people make great products. The only way to develop people to improve processes is by involving everyone in improvement. Andy shares a "T-development model" in which every employee is being constantly coached to grow in two areas: *leadership* and *expertise*. This type of issue has come to the fore with Nina Miah, whose goal of creating just-in-time delivery for Nexplas parts has in fact increased variation rather than leveled delivery.

## Author Comments

On a gemba walk, the sensei will typically point out:

- The safety issues that you think operators can live with because that's the way of work habits.
- The quality issues customers are used to because they're rare or costly to fix and you can't please every body in any case.
- The logistics issues caused by grouping deliveries in order to optimize transport costs, even though that makes them erratic.
- Large batches due to inflexible equipment and long setup times.
- All other unnecessary costs generated by self-created demand variation and vanity investment.

These gemba issues are usually symptoms of much deeper syndromes—difficult technical issues every one is working around. By learning to face and fix these problems, lean thinkers discover the leverage points of the business and learn how to improve step-by-step. Yet, improvement is only the first step to the deeper aim of lean. Each successful improvement effort is the opportunity to develop the people involved on both their technical competences and their ability to work well with others across the value chain.

Collectively, as people are developed in knowing more and collaborating better, they create new capabilities for the organization and cooperate to run better processes. Better people and better processes happen together. Superior performance is the outcome of endlessly improving processes to develop people, and developing people to improve processes. This is not something you can achieve with just a few guys at the top running every one else—you've got to connect every one in the organization to the improvement process.

*Learn to have regular people review and a plan per person to open your eyes to how each person can be developed one point at a time.* The T-model of lean leadership highlights two dimensions of development: deep expertise and leadership (getting others on board and working for you even though you have no authority over them). Regular review of staff on these two dimensions allows the leader to draw a people-based image of the organization and sketch a Plan Per Person: what challenges shall we give each person to grow their expertise and to develop their leadership skills.

## Key Points

- Safeguard your people; protect your customers; control your lead-time; reduce your lead-time; and your costs will go down.
- Process and people are linked:
  Performance = best people + best processes.
- Learning requires a no-fault environment. Punishing the bad failures drives out the spirit of innovation.
- Developing individual competence means learning:
  1) Detailed knowledge of one's job
  2) Understanding how to recognize the waste they generate through choices
  3) An ability to seek root causes and state problems precisely
  4) A knowledge of how to present a set of "solutions" and study countermeasures;
  5) An ability to learn to work better with colleagues.

- Developing others through the challenge aspect of lead with respect creates a constant tension of "teach versus support."
- Managers lead with respect not by designing brilliant processes and hiring capable people to run them; but by developing the expertise of every employee and supporting them in designing their own processes.

## Graphics

### T-development Model

**Leadership:** Solving problems with upstream and downstream colleagues

**Expertise:** Better understanding the fundamentals of the job, and knowing how to deal correctly with specific cases

### Reflection

What lesson(s) have you learned? Please write down your answer.

Can you think of three specific examples that illustrate this learning in your own business? Please write them down.

Do you develop both your technical and leadership skills? How?

Have you had a situation where doing the "lean" thing was not simply counterintuitive, but in fact called for modification based on your unique situation?

What happened?

# Chapter 4: Answers, Notes, Questions

*Chapter Five*

# LEARN TO LEARN

*Establish simple metrics to gauge the effectiveness of improvement efforts at a detailed level.*

Jane and Wembley review the scientific approach to problem-solving with Chris, who now spends most of his time at Nexplas. Chris shares their problem-solving sheet, which links all observed problems to root cause analysis, proposed countermeasures, agreed upon countermeasures, along with a PDCA check. The purpose of the sheet is reflection—a deep thinking sheet. The key part of this practice is confirmation: finding out empirically whether assumptions about which factors cause which problems are true. Doing so requires (surprise) close observation at the gemba with a no-fault mindset, coupled with a structured way of testing hypotheses.

Andy drops by Southcape and runs an impromptu *five why* exercise with a project manager, revealing that the correct cause of a recurring problem is not that the programmer forgot but that there are generic names for their variables which causes folks to overlook them. Later when Jane asks his advice on losing a good employee, Andy counsels her to try to retain him if good, but accept attrition of people as part of the system; that "part of developing people is helping them to succeed in their careers."

Jane agrees to think harder about what it takes to develop people to the fullest of their abilities, treating each person as an individual, practicing catchball, and letting people know how they're doing. She commits to the T-development model personally. And realizes that lead with respect has given her a practical way to manage her firm that she had not seen before.

## Author Comments

If you're committed to lean because you can see the potential, you'll soon learn to get good kaizen efforts going. With CEOs, I often start with a 5S plan: we ask someone to coach a one-shift 5S exercise a week to train every team to improve their own work areas. Lean CEOs commit the time to visit the team at the end of the workshop and recognize what's been achieved, as well as identify some obstacle that they can solve for the team. This usually goes very well.

But does it change anything? It does, at first, when the CEO changes her mind about something by seeing what the teams have done. Any kaizen effort by workplace teams is an opportunity to assess strengths and weaknesses of products or services, people competence and attitude, process effectiveness, and so on. When you ask a team to tackle a kaizen topic, whatever it is, you have an opportunity to learn something from their initiative, if learning is what you seek.

Still, beyond executive education (which is not an indifferent subject, as when the executive changes his mind, all his decisions will change), what has really changed? Not much unless the middle manager in charge of the area where the kaizen has happened learns to integrate the outcomes from the kaizen into their own daily running of their operation.

Getting shop floor teams to conduct kaizen efforts is relatively easy, particularly if you support them with a coach and a program. Learning from their initiatives is a matter of your personal commitment to learning. But getting the business to learn is a question of having the right middle-managers who will pick-up the kaizen ideas and nurture them until policy or procedures is changed. This involves a radically different look at how you staff your organization in order to bridge the gap between individual intelligence and collective intelligence.

*Learn to look at factors one-by-one and clarify the test method of each factor to see the technical leverage points of what you're offering.* Complex problems are often multi-cause and multi-effect. Getting a sense of how impactful various factors are is the way to develop wisdom about complex problems—some things matter more than most. For instance, in lean we have learned that solving rework within a process is the key factor to overall productivity. Similarly, asking for better forecasts is like whistling in the wind, but making production processes more flexible will lead to better deliveries.

To develop insight into such technical, involved issues, we learn to list factors, imagine a specific test method to evaluate the impact of each factor, and test them one by one. In doing so, you will discover that measurement is an integral part of the process and that robust improvement needs a build-measure-learn cycle, not just build-learn.

### Key Points

- The most clever solutions are rarely the best approaches; what most important is revealing how one is thinking.
- What appear to be obvious problems often distract from the true root cause—why improve problems when they can be eliminated?
- Every individual's own development must be viewed individually. Not everyone dreams the same dreams. Have a plan for every person just as one has a plan for every part.
- Setting objectives with employees and then using "catchball" as a way to create meaningful targets together helps align goals and share learning.
- There are two types of kaizen: *problem-solving* (identifying the gap and finding a remedy to get back to standard when standard is known) and *improvement* (working at standard and seeking to be better by identifying the elimination of some form of waste.)

## Nexplas problem-solving sheet

| Date | Problem | Sketch | Cause | Countermeasure | PDCA Check | Status |
|------|---------|--------|-------|----------------|------------|--------|
| | | | | | | ⊕ |
| | | | | | | ⊕ |
| | | | | | | ⊕ |
| | | | | | | ⊕ |

⊕ Problem Identified    ◐ Countermeasure Proposed    ◑ Countermeasure Agreed    ● Problem Solved

## Experiment Confirmation

| Factor | Impact | Confirmation method | Confirmed (Y/N) |
|--------|--------|---------------------|-----------------|
| 1. | | | |
| 2. | | | |
| 3. | | | |
| 4. | | | |
| 5. | | | |
| 6. | | | |
| 7. | | | |

## Personnel Development Matrix

| | Low-improvement effort | High-improvement effort |
|---|---|---|
| Achieve objectives | ? | Stars |
| Miss objectives | Problem cases | ? |

**Reflection**

What lesson(s) have you learned? Please write down your answer.

Can you think of three specific examples that illustrate this learning in your own business? Please write them down.

Would you rather be told you are doing a great job in general, or get credit for your problem-solving efforts?

Do you have a say in setting your own goals with your team leader?

**Chapter 5: Answers, Notes, Questions**

*Chapter Six*

# ENCOURAGE INITIATIVE
# TO DEVELOP LEADERS

*Create suggestion system that engages employees, has metrics for success, and supports lean leadership.*

Jane deals with the internal fallout of gains realized through test-driven development, ongoing worker involvement, and improved customer reports. She challenges her key executives to get on board with this approach—*or go*. She asks her sales director to focus on obtaining good work with good margins, that is recurring and core, and leveled by customer demand. Her accomplishments are further validated when the equity partner says that Southcape's ongoing success has inspired them to acquire a new company its size and consolidate, with Jane in charge.

Andy's operator Stevey shares the importance of standards as the basis for improvement. They are a way for people to know when things are OK versus NOT OK, to have a conversation about the best way to execute—*and improve*—the work. Andy explains the goal of a suggestion program is to encourage initiative. It's about supervisors as much as operators, and needs to have a confirmation stage built-in, so that the ideas are tested and implemented.

Standards and kaizen enable managing for change and organizing for learning. They help with the crucial job of developing new leaders, who learn to face difficult situations and solve problems while keeping priorities. Jane notes how Nexplas structures teams (5–7 people with a leader) and considers how she can build up her own company's organizational capability to solve problems and develop people.

## Author Comments

The business is really nothing more than the sum of every one's contribution, not just the great ideas of the few at the top, executed with discipline, but the sum of the many ideas employees have about their own jobs and how to best achieve what they've been asked (though rarely very clear or oriented towards serving final customers).

Growing the business means recognizing that training direct reports is the first responsibility of every manager. How can people have the right ideas if they're not clear on the business' objectives and known methods to reach them? Recognizing individual initiatives and encouraging their leadership is the second critical skill.

At the gemba on a Toyota line, I once saw all operator kaizen ideas painted in bright yellow to show where operators had improved the line. When Eiji Toyoda describes how he led Toyota, he talks about the systems developed by key executives to grow the business: Kiichiro Toyoda's just-in-time system, Shotaro Kamiya's sales system Masao Nemoto and Hanji Uemata's Total Quality Control system, Taiichi Ohno's kanban system and so on. In his lean vision of leadership, he sees his own leadership of the company as the encouragement and nurturing of other people's leadership and contributions to the total learning system.

*Set up a suggestion system to open your eyes to the potential of greater engagement with all employees.* Suggestions are the aim of the entire system of tools—the system is nothing more than a scaffolding aimed at one outcome: getting people to think, and think about improvement. To start early with suggestions, you need to train frontline managers to accompany suggestions by worker without taking ownership of the ideas brought to them. By creating a board with new suggestion, test area, confirmation by other team members, and adoption in company standards and procedures, the suggestion process can be steered idea by idea, all the way from the original insight to implementation.

## Key Points

- Job = work (with standards) + kaizen
- Standards are the best sequence of steps that describe how we should work now.
- Standards are references, not rules. Because they are the result of collective observation and improvement, they are the best known current way to work. As such they are the basis for improvement; the starting point for kaizen.
- Standards change as people learn to work better and as the line changes in volume, in mix, starts new products, or through kaizen.
- Standards are key to training managers to be able to respond to change; daily problem solving prepares people to face the unexpected.
- Suggestion programs should be designed with motivation and engagement in mind; requests ideas that can be used and which require little investment.
- Visualize processes and react to abnormalities—organizational ability to solve problems—process effectiveness.
- Job satisfaction = engagement + involvement + recognition.

## Graphics

### Operator training sheet

| Step | Operation | Point to watch out for | Idea for waste elimination |
|------|-----------|------------------------|----------------------------|
|      |           |                        |                            |
|      |           |                        |                            |
|      |           |                        |                            |

### Status board

| New suggestion | Confirmation (find a place to test) | Validation (get others to agree) | Standardization (include in standards) |
|----------------|-------------------------------------|----------------------------------|----------------------------------------|
|                |                                     |                                  |                                        |
|                |                                     |                                  |                                        |

### Nexplas organization chart

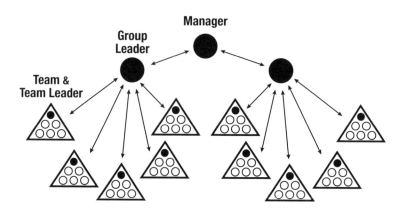

## Minimum job roles at Nexplas

|  | Team Member | Team Leader | Supervisor |
|---|---|---|---|
| Safety | | | |
| Standardized work | | | |
| Remarking abnormalities | | | |
| Kaizen to eliminate waste in the cycle time | | | |
| Eliminate variation in the flow of work | | | |
| Rebalancing the work flow | | | |

## Building up organizational capability

Visualize processes and react to abnormalities

Organizational ability to solve problems

Process effectiveness

### Reflection

What lesson(s) have you learned? Please write down your answer.

Can you think of three specific examples that illustrate this learning in your own business? Please write them down.

How are leadership skills developed at your gemba?

Do you have a suggestion program?

What ways does your company support (or discourage) initiative? Think of examples.

### Chapter 6: Answers, Notes, Questions

*Chapter Seven*

# INTENSIFY COLLABORATION

*Intensify collaboration and mutual trust by using an obeya regularly to review A3s, deepen technical knowledge, solve problems across silos, and boost espirit de corps.*

Jane has a breakthrough moment when she works hard to uncover the root cause of one key employee's recent uneven performance, discovering that his cynicism with the company is mixed in with current personal misery. She offers support without "fixing" his issues.

This exchange causes her to reflect on the key challenge of how she can train her line managers to align the company's needs with employee's needs. She sketches out a "triangle model" and mulls over how to continue to organize for learning with such specific challenges of securing contracts for projects with a level work demand.

Her chief pundit Wembley proudly introduces her to his new initiative of teaching A3 thinking at Southcape. He takes her through the 8 steps of the process he describes as "a structured problem-solving conversation between two people." He argues that while this may sound formal and even mechanical, it is in fact a great platform for innovation—a way to learn and develop basic thinking and teamwork skills. As Jane watches Daniela lead the exercise, she realizes how far her managers have come in terms of embracing teamwork, problem-solving, customer focus, and learning to learn.

The chapter ends with both he and Jane pondering their greatest current challenge: learning to better grow the right talents and leadership fast enough.

## Author Comments

The key to innovation is intense collaboration. Innovation is born of a technical insight and then turned into something real by hard work between two or three gifted people—lone wolves, no matter how brilliant, rarely ever contribute breakthrough innovations.

The much vaunted A3 tool is not so much a tool for solving problems (how can writing problem solving down on paper actually solve anything? To write an A3, first solve the problem, then write it down). It helps to structure one's thinking, sure, but the real value of A3 is sharing one's thought process in an easy to understand format. Try comparing having a discussion with someone about how they solved a complex problem, and sharing with them an A3 storyboard.

To capture collective intelligence from individual intelligence, first you need to encourage middle-management learning from employee's own initiatives, but second you also need the silos to better collaborate to come up with more effective transverse processes. Middle-management A3s is a key tool to sharing problem across boundaries, and, in doing so, create the thinking space to improve the business as a whole by learning from each other's learning experiences.

Developing people's leadership means first developing their autonomy in solving their own problems, certainly, but not less importantly also means developing their ability to convince others across boundaries and carry new ideas through from local beginnings to company-wide initiatives. The leaders we're looking for should both have new technical insights in their domains as well as the ability to share these and bring others along through intensifying collaboration to turn these insights into successful innovations.

*Set up an obeya and have regular A3 reviews to open your eyes to the impact of building self-confidence and mutual trust on overall performance.* Every problem-solving tool can be used to teach teamwork and intensify collaboration. Whether kaizen in a quality circle or a strategy A3, a point person will be given the responsibility for solving a problem, as well as the instruction to work with other key individuals.

"Big Company Disease" expresses itself in the organization by:

1) a disappearance of the final customer in internal processes,

2) solving problems within silos but not taking any interest in solving problems across silos,

3) treating subordinates as an extra pair of hands to execute management thinking—smothering their experience, insights and initiatives,

4) solving cross-functional issues through systems or control structures that keep changing plans, reprogramming work and reorganizing staff, often creating more havoc than they're worth.

There can be no structural or technological solution to Big Company Disease. The only remedy is to take every opportunity to teach people to work better with each other. Every problem solving instance is an occasion to look at the teamwork dimension—how well ideas are exchanged, built upon, and turned into practice.

## Key Points

- Treating each person as an individual, while challenging in practice, will produce better overall results.
- A3 thinking based on idea that a full problem-solving story can fit onto an A3-sized piece of paper. A3 practice tied deeply to lead with respect model and principles.
- A3 works on two levels simultaneously—the author "writing" it to learn and discover and address a specific problem and the boss/coach who steers them through the process, challenges their assumptions, and helps recognize unseen options.
- Supplier relationships go way beyond improving transactions.
- Standards are not rules to be followed but a shared description of the right way to work, even in difficult conditions. One must learn to solve problems in order to apply standards.

**Jane Delaney's triangle of people development**

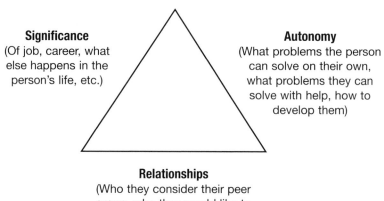

**Significance**
(Of job, career, what else happens in the person's life, etc.)

**Autonomy**
(What problems the person can solve on their own, what problems they can solve with help, how to develop them)

**Relationships**
(Who they consider their peer group, who they would like to work with, what their emotional default mode is)

# A3 Problem-solving sheet

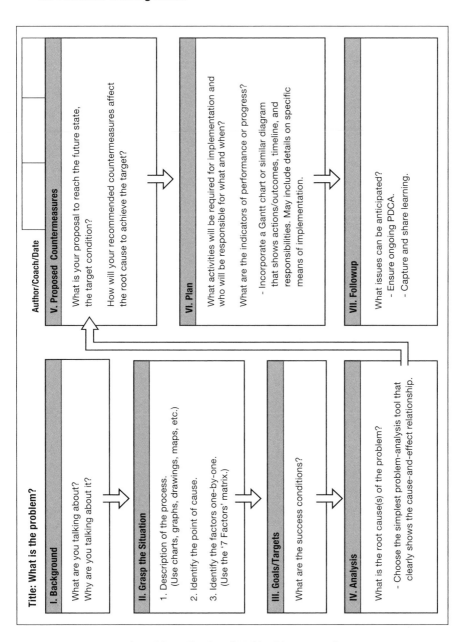

**Title: What is the problem?**

Author/Coach/Date

**I. Background**

What are you talking about?
Why are you talking about it?

**II. Grasp the Situation**

1. Description of the process.
   (Use charts, graphs, drawings, maps, etc.)

2. Identify the point of cause.

3. Identify the factors one-by-one.
   (Use the '7 Factors' matrix.)

**III. Goals/Targets**

What are the success conditions?

**IV. Analysis**

What is the root cause(s) of the problem?

- Choose the simplest problem-analysis tool that clearly shows the cause-and-effect relationship.

**V. Proposed Countermeasures**

What is your proposal to reach the future state, the target condition?

How will your recommended countermeasures affect the root cause to achieve the target?

**VI. Plan**

What activities will be required for implementation and who will be responsible for what and when?

What are the indicators of performance or progress?

- Incorporate a Gantt chart or similar diagram that shows actions/outcomes, timeline, and responsibilities. May include details on specific means of implementation.

**VII. Followup**

What issues can be anticipated?
- Ensure ongoing PDCA.
- Capture and share learning.

Adapted from Shook and Verble, *Managing to Learn.*

### Reflection

What lesson(s) have you learned? Please write down your answer.

Can you think of three specific examples that illustrate this learning in your own business? Please write them down.

How is collaboration built in and supported regarding your work?

How well does closer collaboration with your team members help or hinder better work?

What do you need from your team leader to support better collaboration?

How does this tie into your lean practice?

### Chapter 7: Answers, Notes, Questions

# CONCLUSION

We hope that this guide has helped you adopt kaizen spirit in your daily work. By practicing kaizen every day at the gemba, one acts oneself into a different way of thinking (to paraphrase John Shook). One reminds oneself to put customers first, to listen to frontline employees, to support cooperation across boundaries, to embrace technological changes and, more importantly, to develop leadership in each and every one.

By creating and studying one's own standard work, one learns to chunk work into fundamental units. This, in turn, challenges one to develop the basic skills needed to perform fundamental work well. Asking "why?" further leads us to investigate our own basic knowledge concerning safety, quality, and production techniques in real-life processes. By practicing hands-on kaizen we learn to see how our own routine decisions lead to batching, then to overburden, and in the end generate waste—triggering even worse decisions.

By following us on the journey of this *Gold Mine Trilogy Study Guide*, we hope that you will have started to explore the following facets of your thinking:

- First, discovering with the characters of *The Gold Mine* how to take responsibility for your performance by going to the gemba, learning to see the flow of gold through the process, looking for immediate opportunities to improve, and learning to work with people to try immediately, see what happens, and think deeply to make things better.

- Following with *The Lean Manager*, you will have explored how to create a wall-to-wall management system to support kaizen by focusing relentlessly on customer complaints and trying to figure out the real source of customer problems, by engaging every person in learning through daily problem solving, by creating a sense of clear direction in choosing improvement indicator, and by sustaining the step from local improvement to company-wide improvement in creating the conditions for teamwork and suggestions.

• In *Lead With Respect*, you will have studied how to develop the kind of leadership that will support and expand the management system and turn continuous improvement into a durable competitive advantage. You will have also experimented with specific leadership techniques, such as challenging and listening, teaching and supporting, developing teamwork and learning from team efforts, that will hopefully have made you look differently at the potential of each of your staff and your own relationship with them.

Our wish is that you've had new ideas and conversations with your colleagues by confronting your answers to the questions posed by this guide, and to our take on the various tools and principles. In the end, the growth of any organization rests on the growth of each of its members, through a faster and stronger flow of ideas within and across departments. The flow of improvement ideas is the ultimate source of superior performance as it bolsters both the mindfulness in which standards are performed and the joy of creating new solutions where none was seen before.

This *Gold Mine Trilogy Study Guide* is meant to point you towards the day-to-day opportunities to move things forward at the workplace with the people who do the work themselves. Ultimately, the lean principles and tools are there to lead you to the "aha!" moment when you realize that a specific case is not as you thought and that the person doing the work has a great idea to improve it, one that might lead—with nurturing, support and intense collaboration—to a genuine innovation. This is the greatest promise of lean, and we wish you the joy of it.

# ACKNOWLEDGMENTS

This guide, like all three novels in the *Gold Mine Trilogy*, is made possible by the depth of experience of Freddy Ballé, as well as his uncompromising focus on learning by doing. Michael and Tom thank Freddy for sharing his learning with us, and through these books, a wider audience. Other readers shared invaluable feedback during the creation of this guide. Huge thanks to: Becky Degen, Tanya Doyle, Neil Andal, Dan Jones, René Aernoudts, Marcus Chao, Art Smalley, Chet Marchwinski, Roberto Priolo, Josh Rapoza, Matt Savas, Lex Schroeder, Thomas Skehan, and John Shook.